D0686345

Written in 1927 (published in 1932), José Rodrigues Miguéis *Happy Easter (Páscoa Feliz)* was a potent challenge to the Naturalism which had dominated the landscape of European fiction for a hundred years. This brief novel embodies remarkable insights into personal psychology and remains a literary *tour-de-force*: it has long been celebrated in Portugal and known in Europe as a radical classic. Here it is translated into English for the first time.

The protagonist, vividly imaginative, suffers symptoms of paranoia and schizophrenia. Shut into himself, isolated from the world yet functioning in it, he lives out a fantasy born out of his protest against the humiliation and hostility which have pursued him since childhood. Tragedy inexitably ensues. Yet, in the prison asylum which he finally inhabits, he declares that he has at last found his true self.

Cover based on part of a painting by J. DOMINGUEZ ALVAREZ (1906-1942) Collection of the Calouste Gulbenkian Foundation, Lisbon.

Happy Easter

This book is part of a series: FROM THE PORTUGUESE
1. MIGUEL TORGA: *Tales and More Tales from the Mountain*
2. JOSÉ RODRIGUES MIGUÉIS: *Happy Easter* 3. JOSÉ SARAMAGO: *Manual of Painting & Calligraphy: A Novel*

JOSÉ RODRIGUES MIGUÉIS

Happy Easter

Translated from the Portuguese by
JOHN BYRNE

CARCANET

in association with
CALOUSTE GULBENKIAN FOUNDATION
INSTITUTO DA BIBLIOTECA NACIONAL E DO LIVRO
INSTITUTO CAMÕES

INSTITUTO
CAMÕES

Páscoa Feliz was first published in 1932
Copyright © Estate of José Rodrigues Miguéis

This translation first published in 1995 by
Carcanet Press Limited
402-406 Corn Exchange Buildings
Manchester M4 3BY

Copyright © John Byrne 1995

The right of John Byrne to be identified as the translator of this work has
been asserted by him in accordance with the Copyright,
Designs and Patents Act of 1988

Cover design and calligraphy by Kim Taylor

This book belongs to the series *From the Portuguese*,
published in Great Britain by Carcanet Press
in association with the Calouste Gulbenkian Foundation,
and with the collaboration of the Anglo-Portuguese Foundation.
Series Editors: Eugénio Lisboa, Michael Schmidt, L.C. Taylor

A CIP catalogue record for this book
is available from the British Library
ISBN 1 85754 204 5

The publisher acknowledges financial assistance
from the Arts Council of England
Set in 11/13.5pt Photina by XL Publishing Services, Nairn
Printed and bound in England by SRP Ltd, Exeter

Happy Easter

I

The judge finally bade me rise. 'Have you anything to say in your defence?' he asked, without taking his eyes off the bundle of documents on his table.

He had rather small, piercing eyes, hidden behind thick glasses; his thinning hair straggled across his large, intelligent head. Throughout the case he displayed the same bland indifference with which some priests say mass. I might even say that he seemed not to believe in the effectiveness of justice itself.

The Public Prosecutor affected a high, noble seriousness towards the public in the gallery, who were following the case avidly – not, by the way, because I inspired in them any great sympathy, but because they wanted to hear the whole shameful, dramatic story. What did he say in his accusation? I don't remember exactly: everything was mixed up in empty words and gestures. I only know that he ended by asking that my punishment should be the maximum permitted in this case.

As for the jurors themselves, if they weren't sleeping they were yawning. It's funny but I hardly remember my counsel; there's no point in trying. Poor soul that I am, there is something in my past which remains inexplicable. During the judge's summing up I must have fallen into the kind of lethargy in which I am completely lost to what is going on around me. It is a fact that, since I was very young, certain kinds of self-absorption or torpor have either disturbed me or prevented me paying attention; during them it is as if my spirit abandons me and leaves me in a purely mechanical state.

I shuddered. The judge's question brought me back to

myself. I stood up and put my right hand into the inside pocket of my jacket to pull out the text I had written and which I was intending to read to the court. However, some instinct stopped me in time; instead I got out my hand-kerchief and used it to wipe away the sweat which was running down my face. I left the pages deep in my pocket; after a moment, with my hand hanging by my side I leaned forward slightly: 'I repeat once again that I have committed all the crimes of which I am accused,' I replied in precise, measured tones.

On saying this my heart beat vigorously, with an almost foolish exultation.

'Very well then,' said the judge without looking at me. 'Sit down over there and wait.'

'No, not over there; the other way,' said the bailiff, blocking off one side.

Behind me I heard a sigh muffled by a handkerchief – it was Luisa – and then a hubbub of excited comment. Full of pride, I shot a glance of defiance at the crowd crammed into the court. Wasn't I in truth a rare bird!

I sat down on a bench next to the screen in the midst of the others on trial; they looked at me strangely, full of curiosity. One of them, whom I had never seen before, nudged me and said loudly in a familiar tone of voice, breathing foully over me: 'You'll cop the blame for the whole thing!'

I shrugged, utterly indifferent.

Then there was a babble of voices; the members of the jury rose, stamping their feet on the platform, stretching their stiff legs, and went out through a low door at the end, talking and laughing, bowing extravagantly, while the judge, invigorated, gave instructions to the president of the court. The prose-cuting counsel, in dignified fashion, retired with his briefcase under his arm. In the opening of a window two lawyers with lank hair were debating points of law like two Pharisees, with affected, almost comical seriousness; they smiled as they whispered. On the defence benches, lost in vapid admiration, a dirty, hirsute student was trying to memorise their bearing and gestures. It was my defence counsel!

The clerk of the court did not move from his place: sallow and distraught, he seemed like a dusty, long-forgotten filed-away legal document himself. He kept his thin, discoloured hands under the red moth-eaten cloth on the table, not daring to look me in the eye. I noticed meanwhile that he looked me over from time to time, furtively, with an expression of pious distaste; so I began to stare at him so hard that I made him turn bright red. I laughed to myself and left him in peace.

I'm almost sure that he had me down as a hard-faced cynic.

Time dragged in that room which looked more like a tomb than anything else, with its dusty walls and ancient hand-painted tiled panels with their stylised flowers. From time to time I heard the clinking of the soldiers' swords; a spider, equally indifferent to the miseries and splendours of Justice, was weaving its web in an old gaslight above our heads.

The room smelt foully of sweat, brandy and dust; the heavy, poisonous air was stupefying. The guards dozed on their feet. The murmur of voices rose to a crescendo until the bailiff roared at them to stop and one could hear the buzzing of two flies whirling dizzily above the bald pate of the clerk. The poor man flapped at them despairingly, without conviction; I blew my nose so that nobody would see me laughing.

At that moment a fat, red-faced chap came up to him, whispered something in his ear, slapped him playfully on his scrawny back and disappeared, smiling in self-satisfied fashion at the rabble and waving goodbye on all sides with his pudgy hand. He was a lawyer, well-known in the annals of crime. I supposed that the clerk must be suffering from stomach ulcers as well as problems at home.

In the end all the waiting began to annoy me: why the devil did they have to take so long if the conviction, which I craved from the bottom of my heart, was sure and sound? I thought excitedly of the prison; it was bound to be better than the court. This business, which lacked any semblance of dignity or nobility, all these people, all this incessant toing and froing, the company of criminals, all this deflected me from my keenest and deepest interests. I hadn't even bothered to draft a defence. I was dying to see myself as if from the outside, convicted, locked up forever, free of the world.

My wife was waiting behind me, on the other side of the screen. I turned to look at her and saw her smile through her tears. I think she made a sign but what it meant I couldn't make out. Her eyes were bruised. I shrugged, completely detached, since no sorrow, not even hers, affected me any longer. On the contrary I would rather not have turned to see her, preferring to forget everything and to set out on my new course. For me human sorrow had lost all meaning.

The papers in my pocket had been an attempt to explain what I had done. Don't scoff. I wasn't trying to enlist the sympathy of the court; rather, I wanted to show it that the nature of my crime was so exceptionally complex as to place it above and beyond its glib judgements. I had written it in haste, in gaol, while preparing my case, influenced by the thought of the effect my reading of it would produce at my trial. But what would it matter to those men, indifferent alike to the reasons for my crime and for my composure, which they would only attribute to cynicism.

These citizens want their 'right' to judge another to be as slight a burden as possible. They would have died of boredom, or perhaps they would just have laughed, upon hearing the trifling details of my state of mind. Truth, for these people, is always either risible or corrosive: they start either laughing

JOSÉ RODRIGUES MIGUÉIS

or demanding extra assurances. The only thing that interests the court is an official – relatively so, at least – version of the truth, inscribed in the legal records. At bottom the jurors were stupid of necessity: the spiritual and moral order is hidden from them. Facts! Facts! As far as they are concerned I'd always be just the man who killed in the furtherance of theft.

Suddenly the door at the bottom of the court opened and the bailiff bawled out: 'The court will reconvene. Please rise.'

The judge and the jurors returned to the court; the whole room was full of noise and commotion. I breathed deeply with relief. It was the end of this farce – and for me the beginning of everything. By dint of much jostling and bullying – during which there came the sharp, despairing cry of a child – silence was achieved in less than a minute. The foreman of the jury, bent and fiddling anxiously with his spectacles, read a list of questions and answers in the midst of a deathly silence. The whole room appeared to hang on his parched, pale lips. Behind him, stiff and inscrutable, like altar boys at a funeral, the members of the jury awaited their release. The judge sometimes interrupted the recital in order to clarify matters and I bit my lip so as not to laugh or cry out. At each reply – 'guilty by unanimous verdict' – there was a sudden babble of comment. Finally the judge sat down and, leafing through an old book of statutes, yellowed and full of scribbled notes, began to write out the sentence. The nib of the pen scraped, the pages of the book rustled and an old juror cleared his throat. The fresh scent of orange came to me from the window, like a ray of sunshine. Just as my friend had predicted, I was copping it for the whole lot.

I felt myself pulled to my feet, shaken, led by the arm. A great commotion followed. I can't remember exactly what happened from that moment on: I retreated into myself, as if in a dream fuelled by opium. Everything had seemed to be scoured from my memory and only much later, in gaol, did I manage with a great effort to piece together – and even then imperfectly – what had happened when I was sentenced. There is no doubt that there is something odd about me and so I'm not surprised that these memories come back to me as blurred, shadowy, disjointed, as if it had been another, not I, who had lived through them.

II

I feel fine in this prison. It is a handsome, whitish building, in blocks of two storeys, encircled by a large hedge of trees which is separated by a high wall from, I would guess, paths and cultivated fields. There is no noise from out there. Sometimes I go up to this wall, to which the dense ivy lends a kind of poetry, and in the cool restful shade I give myself up to the sounds of the earth and air – a falling leaf, the trilling of a bird, the humming of an insect, the trickling of water – spending many hours of the day in this fashion, thinking and writing, like the monks of old, until the sound of a small bell calls me to eat or to roll-call.

Everything seems to me unusual, new and extraordinary. I am only now finding out the hidden meaning of many things – and this more by the feelings they arouse in me than by the judgements I make. And so, after all my errors and crimes, I ask myself if it is acceptable to live so calmly and so untroubled: shouldn't a criminal suffer, be tortured? Is this all the punishment there is?

Indeed, I have for a long time felt as though I'm living in a dream. Life proceeds with an astounding serenity. I think how very happy, in another time, were those men who were allowed to flee, as I have fled, the care-ridden life of the world. I could almost say I'm happy. And why not?

Prison is not as I had supposed, nor as those outside believe. We want for nothing. We are well-treated, even though we live in virtually complete seclusion. In any case, this suits me: I abhor the company of men. Only in their outward appearance do I think of them as anything like me. Here I am only a number: number 28.

I can see now how much progress penology has made towards greater freedom: each of us does what he wants – or does nothing. Many prisoners just spend the day in bed. Work has ceased to be obligatory. The rehabilitation of the criminal today, it would seem, works in a more spontaneous fashion, what I would call, if I may, the 'therapy of self-gratification'.

The whole place is immaculately tidy. My room is white and clean, with a high ceiling and a huge window without bars, through which I can see a vast stretch of pine forest and ploughed fields.

I have to record, nevertheless, a very odd fact: sometimes during the night – I sleep little, and lightly at that – I am startled by the sound of cries, quarrelling, groans, the noise of someone struggling, blows and even the shattering of glass. The first time it happened I woke covered in sweat and my hair stood on end. I was afraid they were using the cover of night to dish out some retribution. As things quietened down I began to fall asleep. But it happened again and I ended up thinking I was the victim of some kind of delusion. Why were they crying out? Intrigued, I got up several times to listen, but fortunately I finally found myself losing interest in what was happening in this large mysterious house. Were they prisoners who had kicked over the traces, or were quarrelling, or were they being given a good beating? I don't know. I don't want to know. Nobody gives me any explanation, nor do I seek any. It doesn't matter to me; others don't exist as far as I'm concerned. Let them be like me: quiet, obedient, living peacefully. What use is liberty anyway? Left to his own devices, man simply throws himself over the precipice.

There was another thing which bothered me at first: I'm not allowed to read the papers, not even those which are out of date, where I might read certain facts whose inaccuracies would disturb me.

JOSÉ RODRIGUES MIGUÉIS

What could the mighty press have been saying about me?

I have no news of what is going on in the world; I don't even know where I am. I live like a monk. I like it like this.

What keeps me apart from these people is their fear of being different, of being other.

Oh, this horrible feeling that reality is slipping away under my feet! Laboriously I am putting my 'self' back together, a self that the presence of other people merely dissipates and obscures.

So much is clear and shameful. Often it seems that suddenly I cease to be me, and the idea itself of my crime becomes indistinct. My past is something apart, as if a powerful force has dragged me onto another plane of existence. And so I shrink from and struggle with myself, quite alone, in desperation.

The seclusion and calm of the prison allows me to think more clearly and to organise my many memories. Wrapped up in myself, I can feel my powers of imagination smouldering, vibrant, and I hope I can still put together some volumes of self-analysis and show Nietzsche a thing or two.

Sometimes I think with pity of the insensitivity of those who strive so ardently for a life of freedom. I can laugh at my own past, I who have let myself be seized by remorse and grief. Right now I feel perfectly serene. You cannot imagine what this means to me! Here I am, sitting and writing; I can feel the breath of spring from outside coming through the open window in the rays of the sun, and in the hedgerow I hear the rustle of the newly greening trees which the breeze is softly caressing. Voices... A new sense of exaltation, too, invades my heart.

Almost everyone here has a quite striking respect for me. Only a few of my fellow prisoners, poor souls marooned here, who stroll around like me within the hedge, seem to want to provoke me occasionally. Singular types – being so cut off seems to have robbed them of any sense. The things they say are quite childish and absurd but the watchful guards soon lead them well away from me.

I'm not at all surprised that they are mad if, as I suppose, isolation produces strong reactions even in someone who has always been well-balanced. Solitude is indeed the privilege of the few, the kingdom of the strong! Some of them come up to me to confide in me the most absurd or monstrous things. One of them said he was called Ivano and was a lion-tamer: poor chap, he has rickets and can hardly stand up. Another swore he was Kaiser Bill and is here waiting for the Hindenberg to carry him off to take Paris by storm. I suppose these must be nicknames given to them by the others and around which their overheated imaginations make up stories. Others shout insults or whisper obscenities, tales of amorous goings-on which would make your flesh creep, and which have taken place in here with mysterious women who come from and return to nobody knows where. And there are those who make lascivious and abusive gestures from way off among the trees in the hedge. I simply turn my back on them in indifference. They do not even excite my pity; why doesn't someone throw them in a dungeon?

I don't get many visits and, strange to say, I don't recognise any of those who claim to be relatives of mine. They question me, trot out names, dates and look at me with astonishment and curiosity. Quite frankly, they're a pain. Sometimes I have to be quite abrupt with them. It seems somehow as if I certainly must have known them, but in a previous life of which no living memory remains. I wrestle in vain with these mysteries.

Probably there are those who are interested in my 'case' – novelists or psychologists, who knows? My wife comes too, sometimes in the company of people I don't recognise; it pains me. She looks at me sadly, fearfully, as if I were deranged. She wears black. I'm sure she works to earn enough to eat and her eyes look red and worn. Suddenly she will cling to me, sobbing. 'Remember, remember,' she says.

My God, how these scenes get on my nerves; I can't cope with them any more. I feel as though I'm becoming unbalanced. Just leave me alone! Leave me alone! What do you want me to remember? Why do they all insist that I remember? What – or even who – is there to remember?

So I greet her but without much enthusiasm. If she occasionally surprises me on a day when I'm full of inspiration or I'm working, I just try to get rid of her as quickly as possible. Women somehow imagine that we should sacrifice our highest aspirations to sentimental futility, or to the memory of what is past and no longer exists.

I'm only interested in the present; the past means nothing to me. It's good to go to sleep, certain that tomorrow will be something different. Is the 'I' of today the same as that of yesterday? The past doesn't exist; it's just an idea which we change when we feel like it. Each new day brings a new life.

Everything is finished between us. I feel sorry for her, but why doesn't she divorce me? Women don't understand certain things. If she were to find an honest, devoted husband she could still be happy, and I would be quite content. It's not as if I would be jealous of him. And believe me, I still have a high regard for her. Poor Luisa! I have to be brutally straightforward though she doesn't understand.

The prison governor is very kind to me. I don't know what I've done to deserve it. Some of the attention he shows me is hard to ignore. He goes around in a white coat. Sometimes he asks me questions in a leisurely fashion, and has already managed to remind me of certain things I thought had slipped my mind for ever, perhaps because they were just so trivial. And he does it in such a way that I daren't refuse him.

'Do you see?' he said to me yesterday morning, seated on my bed. 'You've already managed to remember some extremely suggestive bits and pieces. We must continue.' I've promised to show him this document as soon as I've finished it. (It's a rewriting of the one I had in court.)

'That's fine. But take it slowly and write down everything – absolutely everything.'

'I can't,' I reply. 'There are some things I just can't explain.'

'Really make an effort; perhaps I can help you. It's for your own good.'

'But I don't want to leave this place!'

He even wakes me up at night, for no reason that I can discern, just to ask me questions. He shows me pictures, he tells me things which I think I've read about somewhere.

'You've got to recover,' he says. 'By the end you've got to be able to remember everything about yourself.' Then suddenly he asks: 'Who was Abílio?'

I tremble. Abílio... I feel a nameless anxiety.

'Wait, wait. I remember now... I knew someone...'

'Who was he? Where did he live?'

I used to know someone called Abílio, I used to, but I can't make anything out. I want to but there's a wall between me and I don't now what – a dread as if some animal was struggling within me against my will. 'I can't! I can't! I can't!' At the mention of the name I'm completely torn up inside.

'For a month now you haven't recognised this name. And today you do, don't you?'

'I do.'

'Thank you.'

Thank you – why thank you? Why is he interested? Why does it matter to him what is sleeping inside me? I hate it when they ask me these questions.

JOSÉ RODRIGUES MIGUÉIS

I've already suffered. I was a perpetual malcontent, a rebel if that's how they want to put it. Today I live in peace. Serenity is the greatest virtue of intelligence.

What took place within me was simply a struggle between ends and means. Everything that happened to me can be summed up in that phrase. It's not a question of whether I am good or bad: only actions are good or bad, depending on their effects, not on intention. And there are unexpected circumstances, too, which propel us, by way of evil actions, towards a perfectly splendid destiny.

The idea of evil makes me think of society: we're quits, as far as I'm concerned. Society hasn't done anything for me. I owe it nothing, I lived on the edge of it, like a thistle by the side of the road. But I don't blame it either. It's nothing more than an abstraction to which someone who has no expectations can appeal; in fact there are only individuals. (Truthfully, only I exist, I and these thoughts.) And we all want something out of society, don't we?

But what am I doing thinking about the world? It's just a habit; I detest a life of action. Even the gestures I make, the steps I take, are too much for my interior life, the life that is my solace. I want to forget, I want peace. Don't look at me like that, doctor! No more questions! I love this place where I have attained the certainty that I exist because I think.

Why should I bother to lie at this solemn moment when I look back, barely able to contain my feelings, on the story of my life? I am merely the man who did as he was told.

That's no reason to think of me as a criminal, is it?

III

You must not imagine that I am going to tell you the whole story of my life: a life can be told in a couple of words – and if it can't be, then a thousand pages of close-knit prose won't be enough. I would rather, in a concern for scientific – if I can call it that – exactitude, give you a broad picture of a life, the terrain, so to speak, on which this struggle took place, the struggle I am going to tell you about today.

My name is Renato Lima. There's nothing special about the name, except perhaps a hint of poetry or romance, which might give rise to a misunderstanding – in the sense, I mean, of a misleading idea of my personality. In the first place I have no reason, you may be sure, to conceal my real name; why should I, when so many people already know it from what they have read in the newspapers? And, in the second place, names tend to conjure up a certain cast of features, or give the finishing touch to a picture already formed in the mind. Now there's a subject for a thesis! What rules does the choice of a name obey? What obscure reasons govern this choice and how does the choice of a name affect the fortunes of the one who bears it? It's a familiar enough topic, virtually inexhaustible, like all those that preoccupy ordinary people. Don't young girls looking for a husband show a marked preference for certain names? And, if I'm not mistaken, there's more than one popular song devoted to the magical proposition that your name is your destiny, while others sing the praises of the one who bears a certain name. Often, just from the name itself, we build a picture of a person which is quite at odds with the reality – and then we are surprised and even disappointed. Now, as far as the name Renato is concerned I don't know whether it's the subject of any songs but there's no doubt in my case that the name comes from a novel. My mother was just a girl when the local newspaper, *The District of Riomil* (which was where she was born) ran in serial form a tale of political and amorous adventures. 'Renato', the hero of these stories, combined rare, manly good looks with a greatness of soul which led him to indescribable sacrifices and into the most touching situations. Unfortunately the intractable political antagonism between the 'Peg-legs' and the 'Pipe-puffers' (the names given at the time to the worthy representatives of the kingdom's two main parties) stifled the life out of the promising weekly paper at an early stage, and with it perished the Renato of 'Noble Passions'. But my mother kept an abiding memory of him – of which I fell short by some way. I did in fact try several times, without success, to find the book – whose author I didn't know – in the public libraries. I would have enjoyed comparing our fates.

I am thirty-three years old, married and a native of Lisbon. My parents were both from the Beira region; for many years now they have been at rest, somewhere. I know nothing of this obscure family which came out of the earth like the trees and the beasts – and which in the end returned there.

They were humble people. But genealogy was never my strong point. From an early age I learned not to depend on my family – or perhaps it was they who taught me this.

My father worked for a long time in a factory making beer and fizzy drinks. Even today the peculiar smell from these factories overwhelms me with sadness. I remember, too, how noisily he slept; and his rages, when he beat my mother across the back which, resignedly, she turned to him; rages which made me flee from the house, sobbing with fright. He was a poor brute of a man, twisted by his work and by penury, covered in reddish hair, with deep-set, expressionless eyes, to

JOSÉ RODRIGUES MIGUÉIS

which only anger could bring a spark of life. The little he said was expressed in grunts from beneath his dull, drooping moustache. I don't remember him ever smiling or kissing me, talking to me, or caressing me with his gnarled, hairy hand. He never took me out for a walk, as did other fathers with their children. His presence was enough to bring a chill to my heart. But, in spite of all this, I loved him. Strange, isn't it? Perhaps more than anything it was simply the idea of having a father that I loved. It moves me to tears sometimes to see in the street certain men who remind me of him: men selling oil or vegetables, or above all those who sell offal, whose bloodied hands seem always to have something cruel about them. Perhaps it is just a feeling of belated, useless pity.

One day – my father was already dead – my mother was leading me by the hand along a street in the centre of Lisbon when I saw a wagon being pulled at a trot by a horse. I don't know why, but I thought I recognised my father, and slipping my mother's hand I began to run down ,the Rua dos Fanqueiros shouting wildly, 'Father, oh my father! Oh daddy!' So many people were moved by the spectacle of this little boy who, perforce, needed his father. My mother, in distress, ran after me, trying to make me see reason. In the end the man realised that the cries were directed at him (or perhaps someone signalled to him); he, pulling at the reins, turned the horse round to face me and held out his arms. Moved, he sat me on his lap and carried me round the Terreiro do Paço in his cart. Amazed, safe in his arms, this was the first time I had kissed my father – this man that I did not know. When he lifted me down to the ground beside my mother the cart driver asked whether she wanted to sell me. 'You see, I've already got six children,' he said. My poor mother recoiled in horror and I was left fatherless again.

My mother starched clothes for other people, took care of the house and of me, cooked when the occasion demanded, running back and forth to the houses of her customers, to the pawnshop, to the shops, talking to herself, sometimes crying as she sat in the kitchen. The only thing she didn't do was rest, because rest, that difficult business, seemed not to be part of her destiny. I always see her with lines of suffering and anguish on her pale, smooth face, a face I now know was old before its time.

Among our 'relations' was a town Councillor who lived on Rua do Salitre, in a house with carpets and palm trees in flowerpots on the stairs, who would come to play an important part in my life. And in fact the only function of these councillors was just that – to assume roles of some importance in the eyes of the simple and the humble.

My hair is black, shot through with white, and these days I have it cut very close. I was never particularly likeable or pleasant. It was always a torment to see myself in the mirror: my face is badly proportioned, my eyes are too wide apart and my ears stick out. Indeed, if a pleasing appearance helps us to go far in the struggles of life – as I used to think – then certainly I owe my failure to those features which have marked me out. There's no doubt that men look down with contempt and malice on the ill-favoured. I have experienced it often enough; on top of everything else my squint has only made things worse.

At school my ears were pulled mercilessly. Could that have made them so big? I was seven when an old woman, who had come to visit my mother, was stroking my head.

'My fine boy,' she said, 'your little ears are so big. You're going to be very rich. Big ears are a sign of good fortune!'

With my huge ears I waited for that stroke of luck which never came.

Some days ago in the governor's office I caught a glimpse of myself in the mirror. I found the sight of myself painful and

JOSÉ RODRIGUES MIGUÉIS

repugnant, with my narrow shoulders thrust forward, my hollow chest and wan complexion.

Anyone who looks at me will soon see the sad, pale little boy that I was, beaten down by the blows which an unfathomable destiny heaps upon shy, helpless children. It was for this reason, undoubtedly, that I used to believe so fervently in God and His saints. I put up with the coarse whims of brutal school-fellows and suffered the indifference of teachers and prefects, an indifference as towering as the arches of the aqueduct of Águas Livres.

Not a single person ever looked at me with tenderness – except my mother whose eyes always glistened with tears. From an early age, therefore, I stored up the desire for a tenderness I had never known as well as dreams of revenge.

One day at school a girl pinched me and, running away, shouted: 'So long, half-wit!'

'Hey, half-wit! Half-wit!'

A gale of laughter filled the school. My snack of dry bread slipped from my shaking hands. In my confusion I turned red right in the middle of the huge, excited throng among which I could see a hundred, two hundred, mouths open, their teeth showing in derision. I tried to run away, to break through the solid barrier. It was impossible: I was kicked, shoved, covered in scratches and spit, like a Christ. I rolled on the ground. I sobbed, with my face hidden in the dust. I had gone down to hell, burning with hate and shame.

'Hey, half-wit! Half-wit!'

That childish laughter suffused everything, overflowed everywhere, imbued my whole existence. From then on I was always the 'half-wit'.

When some of my more sensitive schoolfellows, out for a stroll, passed me in the street, they would look at me in a kindly, pitying fashion which irritated me horribly, and would say beneath their breath to their parents or brothers and sisters: 'Look, there goes the "half-wit".'

Others even hounded me in the street, crying: 'So long, "half-wit".'

When my mother got to know that I had been dubbed the 'half-wit', her distress caused me to suffer like nothing else. I sobbed all night long with my arms around my straw bolster. At least this object, although indifferent, neither insulted nor rejected me. And for me there could be nothing more cruel than the idea that my mother had been made to suffer. Womankind, which in her was to be revered, and seemed almost divine in its humility and love, now came to be seen as cruel and hostile in the form of the girls at school.

I was a solitary boy, tormented by bullying on all sides. Caught between laughter and scorn, I did not immediately pour all the passions and feelings of an unhappy child into hate and rebellion. Rather, I shut myself away in dreams. At about this time my father died, killed in an accident at work. They found him at the bottom of a vat of beer, his skull cracked open.

'Get lost, go home, half-wit,' they called, throwing stones at me.

'You'll pay for this,' I replied, choking back my tears.

I soon forgot about vengeance and began to weave daydreams in which I was the commander and the others merely soldiers. They were never made to pay in any form at all. Soon I became convinced that injustice is the law of life. They were destined for a life of ease, to start wars, and to play quoits or at being messengers in the grassy countryside where today they are building so many of these nondescript apartment blocks. I couldn't fight like them, nor run so quickly, nor throw stones so accurately. As an enemy I was contemptible; as an ally, a liability. They didn't bother to fight me: I just looked on at them from a distance.

When I was twelve I lost my mother in a typhoid epidemic. They took her off to hospital and I never saw her again. I waited for her at home for two days. On the third day a policeman came with a piece of paper. He took me to the station, gave me something to eat and, when they asked me if I had any family, I remembered the Councillor in the Rua do Salitre, who had a carpet and flowerpots on the stairs.

They took me there. I went in through the servants' entrance and waited. The Councillor gave me a few pence, perhaps what he owed my mother for the starch she had applied, on many a stifling night, to the high collars he wore on ceremonial and state occasions. Quaking, I pleaded with him not to send me to the workhouse. He smiled. And so I stayed to eat with the servants in the kitchen, and sleep in the garret. From its oval windows I could see, far off on the Tagus, the sailing boats gliding over the bright azure waters. The servant girls laughed at me, calling me 'the little savage' and plied me with soup, soup which deadened the hunger of many years. There was something compassionate about these girls, in their suppressed motherliness, even in their off-hand rebukes, which brought me comfort.

'So what are we going to do with this gift?' asked the Councillor one day, twisting my ear in a paternal fashion. I shrank into myself in confusion. 'What can you do, boy?' he inquired.

Not a word could I say. The servant girls around me giggled. 'He eats like a beast,' they said. 'God bless him!'

I knew well that without the bitter seasoning of humiliation there would not be any soup for the poor of this world. 'Can you read, or write?' asked the Councillor. 'And what about arithmetic; can you do your tables?'

Blindly I seized the pencil someone was holding out and, without a word, glad to be able to show that I could do something, I began to add up, divide, multiply in haphazard fashion... In my haste I think I got everything wrong.

'I want you to learn these tables well, do you hear?' said the Councillor. 'If you don't have them off by heart when I ask then you'll only have slops to eat. You know what slops are?' he concluded, not quite stern, not quite laughing. He had already been Civil Governor.

He gave me a few pennies to buy a book of tables at the corner shop. I chose one with a violet cover. And every day, seated in a corner of the kitchen, while the maids laughed, whispered about men or sang noisily, I lost myself in my tables and in my dreams. In any event I felt safest there, in the heat and the tempting aromas of the kitchen.

The Councillor was a widower and had a son in the army, who spent long periods away from home. On his return he never failed to visit the kitchen where he could be with the girls. 'Look, master,' they said, giggling, 'your dad has got himself another son. And he's daft, poor thing!'

They shrieked hysterically, crying with mirth, and the lieutenant, vaguely puzzled, smiled. He looked at me as if seeking some resemblance to his father in my features: but the inspection left him dissatisfied with me, and in his disgust he pulled a wry face. I was afraid of him, his uniform scratched me and seemed designed to keep me at a distance. The maids talked of this young gallant all the time, with a maddening persistence – about the girls he knew, his parties, about the diseases one could catch in the places he went to with one or other of those girls.

Every Sunday, on the Councillor's orders, I went to Mass with the maids. My belief in God and the saints was quite spontaneous and personal; heaven and hell had not sprung from my imagination. But the churches were cool in the stifling days of summer, and this attracted me – this and the solitude and the marble echoes, the gloomy torch-holders and the intricately carved gold altars, the tiled panels and the

JOSÉ RODRIGUES MIGUÉIS

impassive effigies, the music and the artificial flowers. I even managed to weep with rapture during certain parts of the sung Mass. So it was not hard for me to assume the outward appearance of a true believer. In any case I knew the price of my bowls of soup. It was a way of staying alive.

The Councillor put in a good word on my behalf with the priest, who was short and fat, and getting on in years; one leg was shorter than the other and he wore a shoe with an immensely thick sole. He liked me, nuzzled the thin nape of my neck, and led me with a paternal hand through the byways of the Catechism.

At one point he even took me behind the high altar and to the shadowy nooks and crannies of the empty sacristy; when he cleared his throat it resounded in the silence like the trump of doom. There he instructed me in the teachings of the Church.

Anxious to please the Councillor, I made impressive progress in the Commandments and Theological Virtues, even as far as the chapter on Mortal and Venial Sin. It was not so different from school except that I was sheltered from the blows of this world: there were no rowdy boys to make fun of me, no louts to bully me, no one looking out for me with sticks in their hands, like the boy they called 'Scabbardfish', who, though I had done no wrong, made me pay for the mischief of others. Everything seemed to move in an atmosphere of transcendent mystery and grace, which excited my curiosity without affecting me in any other way. I even began to serve at Mass though my voice was not really up to it.

One day the curate suggested to the Councillor that I take holy orders. 'With the head on him that he has, he should go far...' he said.

The Councillor raised his eyebrows: 'Arithmetic, arithmetic, that's what he needs! More work!' He was a liberal, preferring the First Reader to the Catechism.

After Mass, in good weather, the maids would take me for a walk in some public garden, where there was always a military band on the bandstand. There they took advantage of their leisure and of the music to meet some oafs, sometimes in uniform. They whispered and giggled a great deal, while the oafs latched onto them, wanting to prolong their conversation.

'Look at that layabout!' they would say. 'Are you going to tell everything to that idiot?' I pretended that I was listening to 'The Soul of God'.

At night the Councillor would call me to the dining room, which always frightened me with its gloomy furniture, convoluted and sinuous; belching, and with a toothpick stuck in his moustache, he would ask: 'Seven times seven? Nine times six?'

I gave him the answers all the wrong way round, glancing at him out of the corner of my eye, just to see what would happen. He looked at me mistrustfully, unsure of himself, trying to find the book of tables, which I had hidden. 'Eh? Are you sure?'

I realised that he knew nothing about arithmetic, and secretly rejoiced. (This pillar of respectability would one day become the Secretary to the Treasury.) Finally he called me, in paternal fashion, a donkey. 'Off you go now to the kitchen; they'll give you something to eat,' he added. 'You're just hungry, my boy, that's all!'

I left the dining room with my head bowed and my mouth watering. But I knew I had the knack, above all else, of mental arithmetic.

One fine day some time later I found myself working in a shop in the street, on condition that the owner let me attend night school. I moved out of the garret and kitchen. Sometimes the maids came running to see me. 'And what about the lazy-bones,' they asked the owner, 'how's he doing?'

Out of regard for his customer, and since I did not receive a wage, just bed and board, the grocer gave me a candle so that I could read in bed. It was a happy time. At first I was afraid of the mice which abounded in the shop and in my attic. Later I got used to them and they kept me company. Some of them began to eat out of my hand. When the master had taken away the ladder which led to my little den and I closed the trapdoor I felt like a lord in his feudal castle.

I noticed that the grocer gave short weight in the goods that he sent to my benefactor's house, but I never uttered a word: I don't know why, it just seemed to me right that the Councillor should pay more than the poor for the salt cod, the rice and the olive oil which the grocer offered his customers. My master was from the provinces, hated the priests, the monarchy, councillors, the inspectors, and treated them all as if they were a pack of thieves. But when, from the door of the shop, he saw the Councillor alight from his carriage he bowed and scraped and dissolved in smiles.

'Isn't Your Grace sending the boy to Mass?' asked the maid.

'Don't come to me with any nonsense about priests and Masses,' he shouted. 'Bunch of rogues! It's all right for you lot who just love men in skirts!'

At these sacrilegious words the women fled through the door, scandalised; and, laughing, called him a heretic, saying that they would have to tell their master everything. 'Let them, the sluts,' snarled the grocer. But when they returned he gave them dried figs and other titbits. From him I learned to dupe the inspectors and to boost takings. One day the Councillor paused by the door of the shop asking for me; Sebastião grabbed me by the scruff of the neck. 'He's a good, quiet boy, faithful too; he's good for business too,' he added.

'He's a good little beast of burden, yes indeed sir!'

The Councillor gave me a small coin and left majestically, his huge backside swaying between the sacks of potatoes and rice.

Little by little I ceased to see him. There was always a carriage at his door with a servant in livery and braided cap: this was the minister's personal courier who spent hours seated on a step, reading the paper, and from time to time he slipped furtively through the servants' entrance.

When, two or three years later, after the death of my master – which happened in some place I'd never heard of during the riots – his heirs threw me out onto the streets; I was alone again, so I knocked on the Councillor's door. The windows were all shut up and lined on the inside with dull grey paper. The Republic had just been proclaimed, and a maid I didn't know, dressed in mourning, told me that the councillor was abroad somewhere, on account of the disorders and the shooting. That was the end of that episode. Henceforth I would live alone, looking out for myself. I never saw anyone from the house again.

The imagination is, in truth, a dangerous and seductive draught. For me it was now a haven just as if I had, in a large, crowded house, discovered the gate to a secret, silent garden which was my very own domain. Life passed me by, unable to deprive me of this knack I had of raising myself above things. (Even the death of my mother did not affect me quite so severely as I had feared.)

I would await with concealed ardour the lonely hours of night, there in the silent darkness, to transform my nervous exaltation into a delirium of fancy.

Life out there had nothing to do with my dream. I hated any contact with people and everyday dealings. In the intoxication of my imagination, however, I moved among people, I

JOSÉ RODRIGUES MIGUÉIS

did things, I was somebody in the social world of my desires. Hardly had I switched off the light when from all sides thronged a mass of images, of intrigues, of adventures. Some were very dear to me – and I spun them out or repeated them night after night. I lost myself in the burning images, setting out on mad adventures, or for a love that in reality could never have been mine. I had inexhaustible riches, the greatest in the world. I controlled everything, I wore the golden splendour of glory. In bloody battles I was mounted on high-mettled horses, my sword gleamed as it whirled and cut a furrow of death and terror in the enemy ranks. I fought, I conquered, I dominated. I bestrode conquered cities to the sound of trumpets, among vivid, waving banners and the frenzied crowds. I was, by turns, cruel, magnanimous and passionate. The most beautiful women, languid, indifferent, naked, became, when I carried them off to my impregnable castle, faint with desire in my arms, dazzling, drunk with passion, their red mouths half open, their eyes wild, their breasts provocative and their hair hanging loose.

I loved with a licentious passion these shadowy women with whom my dreams peopled the obscure life of my senses. I only needed to stretch out my arms in the dark to hold them and possess them; my taut hands grasped shadows, my body shook and became contorted, while I murmured tender words, kissing ghostly mouths until sleep and exhaustion overcame me. Morning would find me cast down, the scales fallen from my eyes, hating my existence even more. Poor, sad child, my instincts overflowing wildly, I had been touched by the magic wand of imagination and by the fickle, glowing red flower of desire.

Life would never again yield victories like these, nor any stronger excitement. Reality, even when satiated by love, was always poorer than my dreams; nor was there ever the body of a woman which could quicken me so intensely or so deeply as those of which I dreamed in solitude, during the long sleepless nights of puberty.

My memories of this time are confused and tumultuous. Naturally I have tried to forget how I suffered. I know that I hated the struggle, the scramble for prizes. Life repelled me, ruinous and violent as it was for the poor. Even my bread was bitter. I wanted something which I vaguely suspected life could offer. In contrast to what I think today I used to say to myself that my suffering was the fault of others.

I truly wanted to love someone, to be happy, to make someone happy; but the bitterness of life infected all my thinking and acting. 'Joy and goodness are the prerogatives of the strong,' I thought. Nevertheless, I now realise that I was not, in certain aspects, less happy than many of those I envied. In fact I never really aspired to anything in particular. My life was a vague longing, nameless and sad. But I got on with it. I was honest and sober. My work was praised. My soul, however, was above all this. Later I used to go to a modest café where I would read the paper in the evening, listening to the laconic voices, the laughter of the players and the sharp smack of the balls on the billiard table.

I worked in many shops and offices, but erratically in a way I can't explain. On some days I was seized with a sudden need to kick over the traces, a longing to be free, to be my own boss, to run through the streets heedlessly, to breathe to the full the fresh, salty air there on the quays, to climb Lisbon's hills and spend hours up there looking at the horizon, the irregular line of the mountains, the whimsical and elusive rows of houses, the river flowing languidly to the sea. On those days I refused to carry out even the simplest order. Any remark would drive me into a rage. I wasn't going to be under anyone's thumb. 'The boy is mad,' they would say, and I would clap on my hat, say good afternoon and never return.

JOSÉ RODRIGUES MIGUÉIS

I felt that I was another person. My sinews were made of steel. Sometimes I responded to criticism with insults and even with blows. Where did I get the strength from?

At that time there were a lot of gold coins around. One afternoon I had a short, violent quarrel with a book-keeper, my superior, whom I otherwise admired. Nearby someone was counting money and stacking coins on a large table. In an access of rage I seized the table and overturned it so that the coins spilled onto the wooden floor, crashing and clinking, to be lost under the furniture and down the cracks.

They said I was mad, as the others had done. But after these wild outbursts of rage my life seemed to have a savour of infinite freedom and joy. I would spend days just wandering around, sleeping where I could, eating in cheap taverns or restaurants, alone, using up my savings. Otherwise I was self-effacing. I was a good employee and so I soon got myself another job when boredom or the need for money or some occupation demanded it.

And so I lived for many years, working while my youth imperceptibly slipped away.

Without doubt something had changed in me: at bottom, though, I still felt the same. But this isn't important, not even the banal story of a marriage.

I am, then, a man who spent the best years of his youth bent over desks in dark, cramped offices of doubtful cleanliness, keeping the books, and writing letters in which I had not the slightest interest. My destiny was to obey. And thus life in every way conspired to push me towards the solitary isle of dreams.

I V

I was poor when I got married, but marriage improved my state of mind. I almost began to think I was happy, knowing that someone wanted to be with me, and even share with me, in a resigned sort of way, a humdrum life without much future. I had stability and I managed to fix myself up with work with a certain Nogueira, an affable sort with a shiny bald pate and gold-rimmed glasses. After a while there was even a kind of fellow-feeling between us which made me forget the distance which truly separated us. For he was rich. I don't know how – drawing together various strands, I now believe it was some sort of shady deal – but he had made a handsome fortune in Manaus, where he had lived for more than thirty years. His clientèle was good, though not numerous. They did solid, worthwhile business, according to principles which had fallen into disuse since the political crisis. We worked together more like comrades; he was never out of countenance with me and his good humour seemed inexhaustible.

'Why, sir, are you working like this,' I asked him one day, 'if, as it seems, you can afford not to?'

He shrugged and smiled: 'My friend, I simply don't want to die of boredom. You just seize up if you don't do something. How do you want me to spend my time and money, old and single as I am?' In serious, almost sad vein, he continued: 'Doing nothing would be the end of me: I'd just curl up there in a corner. I've been saving up a few... Someone would only come and get his hands on it. And, anyway, work helps us forget so many things!'

'That's exactly the way it is,' I replied.

I inclined my head. Perhaps for me too work was a mask behind which I could hide my feelings.

The business was on the quay, on the first floor of an old building, with low wooden ceilings and yellow walls with tiles along the bottom. Carts and wagons thundered over the uneven surface of the street all the blessed day; it smelt simultaneously of livestock, of charcoal smoke, of the sea, of the fish being fried in the taverns alongside – and of the mustiness of the office, too. From the nearby workshops and warehouses there came the clang of metal; the metal chains of the cranes on the quayside grated and creaked. The noise of all that work filled my ears – the whistles of the factories, spirited and strident, and the sombre, gruff foghorns of the steamships, which made the windows rattle. On certain foggy mornings on the river the noises of the packets and cargo ships, coming and going with their characteristic evocative bellow, made me feel with a sudden sharpness that I was forgotten, beyond the pale; I felt a dread of having been left behind and a craving to be on the move, to carve out an opening for myself towards new worlds. My longing to be away became heavy with the knowledge of a lassitude that was holding me back from those dreams of adventure and travel which I had had as an adolescent.

Passing the smithies and forges I stopped and peered inside with childish curiosity: they were caverns of hell, full of shadows and flickering light, where great monsters of men, blackened and red, struck starry sparks as they hammered at the anvil. Force, violence... the brutal work of those men gave me the idea of a great poem about work – which I never attempted or even sketched out – and made my small, mean figure even smaller and more insignificant. I envied those men who, with their powerful muscles, created shape and movement.

JOSÉ RODRIGUES MIGUÉIS

Meanwhile I applied myself to my work, outwardly calm – perhaps more from irresolution and the anticipation of future prospects than from true serenity.

Gradually my attention to detail, my punctuality, and my professional know-how, gleaned from experience, won me the confidence of my employer. He gave me responsible jobs to do. In time I became not simply a book-keeper; I was virtually a manager. Nogueira let me give orders; he took my advice and listened to me before making important decisions.

Nothing much happened in the office. Apart from the boy from the warehouse there was a youngster who helped me. Every day there were long hours of solitude. Only the sound of the typewriter broke the silence, chattering away under the uncertain fingers of the clerk there in the entrance hall. The bell on its carriage sounded from time to time, thin and sharp; a pause, then the carriage was returned with a dry thud. And once again the slow, hesitant chatter of keys.

I can still hear the discreet tick of the round, black dust-covered clock, almost forgotten up in the roof.

And so I worked for five, six years, maybe more, I'm not exactly sure – not that it matters. All these memories are like a chain, a chain of days, all alike. I stopped noticing even the passage of time. My life could not have been more commonplace; I felt myself falling sleep.

My undefined and aimless longing had subsided after my marriage. The state of matrimony is a sedative, an opiate, it reduced one to conformity. I felt incapable of either good or bad. My life became so mechanical that I would not even stoop to pick up a wallet and return it to the person who had lost it, not even if his life depended on it. But I was equally incapable of picking it up to keep it for myself.

As time passed, however, while I wrote letters and drew up columns of figures, to the sound of the never-ending, dutiful scraping of the pen, something began to happen. Like a cloud thickening, in that atmosphere of confused agitation, perhaps because of the somnolence of the place – I don't know which – there began to form within me, of its own accord, in a world apart, a plan, the idea of something novel and extraordinary: a coup.

It was, at first without any great misgivings, that I witnessed the birth of the 'plan'. It was a friend, a guest who settled down with me and whom I did not try to get rid of. Why should I not admit it? It awoke in me an interest in the curious journey on which my subconscious had embarked.

The idea unfolded rather as do landscapes or the features of a face: first of all, vaguely, then in the details which our curiosity uncovers, little by little, bringing them together to form the whole.

A panorama spread out before me repeatedly, each time in greater detail.

My pen followed its own path over the smooth surface of the paper, across the vertical lines, red and blue, bringing order to the numbers and signs. It was as if I were gifted with second sight as, within me, I pursued the progress of my plan, the growing particulars of which surprised me. It was truly a spontaneous gestation. Every day there was a new task to occupy me: now cooking the books, now forging a deposit note, then a cheque. And so it went on, perfect, logical, orderly.

'What a wonderful day,' said Nogueira, coming into the office.

'Splendid, isn't it?' I replied.

'Working hard then?'

'Yes, I suppose so.'

'Good,' said he. 'I don't suppose there's anything I can do?'

'No, nothing.'

'That consignment for Bonfils?'

'It's on its way,' I replied.

'Good, and the Baptista Brothers' account – is it already...'

'Closed? Yes; it's been sold for 7,936 escudos and twenty centavos.'

'And twenty? Wonderful; I'm off out.'

I didn't raise my head. As his confidence in me grew, Nogueira began to appear less and less often. He would come late and then go out 'to take the air'.

It used to hurt my kidneys always to be standing, bent over my desk. How many times the pain had annoyed me! At other times I had used the excuse of some duty down the street just for a change. But this new enthusiasm rid me of all weariness and pain.

I would arrive at the office, hang my hat perfunctorily on its hook, take off my coat and, donning a dust-jacket, immerse myself in my work and in my plan. It kept me company, it was a delicious game which animated me more and more. As far as I was concerned reality was as different from that dream as day was from night. I felt as if my intelligence was controlling everything.

My work was swift, accurate and completed on time. My dream gave me an extraordinary power to get things done. Nogueira was amazed at the laconic clarity of my observations, of my plans, at the precision of my way of working.

'How can you be working alone like this?' he said. 'Everything always on time, everything so clear! What a man!'

He clapped me on the back in friendly fashion.

Indeed, I was under nobody's thumb. And the business prospered.

How can I explain all this? Those emotions which had marked my puberty were the only ones comparable to those of this astonishing time. Never, since childhood, had I felt an exaltation inside me to equal that of this dream which now consumed me so completely. I was planning a theft, to be carried out at length, carefully, patiently. Why? Could anybody explain those dreams which seem to us to be perfectly logical and which upon waking leave us feeling vaguely troubled and with an impression of their meaninglessness?

That's just how it was. Dreams are the domain of madness within reason. Beyond our common logic there is another, deeper, logic which only madmen are in touch with.

In the end my whole body throbbed with a mysterious longing – the longing for a power unmatched, transcending all, which would finally be my undoing. But only now do I use that word. And, oh, though I am ashamed to say it, I had fallen into a kind of criminal onanism. Nothing beyond my dream interested me. I gave myself up to its intoxication for hours every day, only emerging to see to an important customer, sort out some matter of moment or exchange a few words with Nogueira. He used to come back in the middle of the afternoon, his face wreathed in smiles and sweating profusely. 'Any news?' he would ask.

He would roll a Brazilian cigarette and soon the unmistakable aroma would fill the place while I turned to face him, forcing myself to listen to him and his plans, with my pen stuck behind my ear and my left hand in my belt while I supported myself with my right hand on the desk. Exchange rates, Brazil, where he was thinking of going for the last time to wind up his affairs. Brazil was for him still that distant land, almost primitive, a country of fevers, gold and black men and women. As we spoke, my tone of voice, so calm, astonished me after the inner turmoil which had just gripped me.

'Renato, you're working too hard... I'm telling you, now!' he said.

'No, no, not at all. Too much, me?'

(The 'half-wit'! Now they knew what the 'half-wit' could do, that dead-loss of other days.)

'In fact, Mr Nogueira, work gives me a great boost,' I said. 'I'm a lot brighter and happier when I'm working.'

It makes my flesh creep to remember the depths to which my soul had sunk. I used to smile to myself sometimes at that restless need to contrive such adventures. 'How,' I used to think, 'can I rob this kind, simple man who shows such concern for me and for my life? This man who has shown me a better future – no, what a hare-brained idea! You would be an utter wretch. But it's just a dream, no more than my imagination.' It affected me so much that I wanted to embrace him and kiss him as if he were my father. I regretted my wicked actions which would end up, in my mind anyway, ineffectual, harmless. But like certain addicts I experienced at once both revulsion and pride in my addiction. 'This is all the result of too much reading,' I would say. 'It's just my fanciful nature!'

When I got home in the evening, returning to real life worn out by my obsession, it was as if I was re-emerging from the frozen immobility of a dark fastness into the light: I cracked my knuckles, stretched out my arms, and my spirit returned to the things of this world, real and everyday.

V

For a long time I only thought about my scheme during the calm of the working day. There, in the office, I seemed to all intents to be completely in control of myself. I did not take my imaginings home with me, and sometimes I felt that I was possessed of an equilibrium, a power, of an astonishing lucidity. I suppose you could say that my dream was the abscess into which all my instinctive evil was poured.

I was earning well and my life improved: I moved to a flat on the fourth floor in the Avenidas Novas where the air was good and the sun shone, to get away from the old places, dirty and diseased, where I had spent my childhood – not that I didn't have sweet, precious memories of them. I refurnished the house with more style, I bought books and even spent some of my savings on an outing or two.

'Why all this?' Luisa would say. 'We've been living so happily, so well, in our modest way. Anyway, I don't like outings; I prefer my little house.'

'They'll do you good. And the little boy needs them.'

'When I'm bored I just go to the window,' she said. 'There's no lack of fresh air and sun.'

She kept the habits of her poverty, economising and thinking fondly of her son's future. 'With what you've paid for this furniture you could educate the little one. Such extravagance.'

Wiping away a tear of regret she watched an old mahogany sideboard, with its ornamental carving of leaves and fruit, being taken away, as well as our oval dining table. 'Shouldn't we keep this? Who knows, one day...'

'Don't be daft. Anyway, what do you know about the future?'

As for me, I had not the slightest idea of the future. But I always preferred to break abruptly with the past. From time to time I would open drawers and spend hours tearing up papers, notes, things I'd begun to write – all the detritus that time leaves behind in the life of a solitary man like me.

'Oh, not this, don't throw this out,' she would cry. 'It's so lovely.'

It might have been a print, a doll, a drawing I had made at school. 'What do you want with this? Memories...' I shrugged while Luisa ran to hide the thing in her own drawer.

'I loved our train set so much,' she said. 'We were so happy.'

'But we are now, aren't we?'

'Oh!'

'All right then, don't sell it,' I said. 'Have we anywhere to keep it?'

On impulse she kissed me, blushed and then thanked me.

Nogueira continued to be more than satisfied. He let me have the keys to the safe and increased my share of the profits. I began to sign almost all our correspondence. I picked up the indelible pencil and – scratch, scratch.

'Well, now you're the lord of all this,' he said, as we laughed together. 'One of these days we'll have to draw up a deed.'

He nourished his plan to quit the business once and for all to go and live on a farm in the Minho, far from Lisbon, where he might end his days as he had begun them – among trees and beneath a patch of blue sky. He spoke to me often about his dogged days of struggle. Through his words I caught a glimpse of a corner of the lands of the Amazon – the alligators, the tangled forest, the Igarapé snake, which everyone who had been to the Amazon said they had come across.

'I sat down on a tree trunk to rest and eat a bite, I took off my big hat, and because my knife was sticking into me I took it out of my belt intending to bury it in the thick bark of the tree trunk. If you could have seen! Suddenly, as soon as the knife touched it, I felt the tree move and I heard the half-breeds crying out, "The snake, sir, the snake!" and they fled, leaving me behind. I had sat down on an Igarapé snake. I just ran and I didn't stop until I was miles away.'

But he never let slip more than that. What had he been doing there? How had he come by his fortune? On his hands, which were coarse, the hands of a labourer, his diamond rings presented a striking contrast. I looked at him.

'I've done what I had to do; we can't go back,' he said. 'I need to rest; I'm getting on for seventy, and as for the time that's left to me...'

He still had a Brazilian accent. I replied that I thought he looked vigorous and youthful.

'That's just a matter of appearance. When you least expect it, that's when the devil comes and takes you away.'

He had in mind to pass the whole business on to me, bit by bit, just keeping part of the profits for himself.

The ease with which the outer part of my plan was being carried out scared me. I couldn't call a halt now. I was overwhelmed by its momentum. The certainty that I would, one day, be the rightful owner of that business, did not lessen my desire. On the contrary, Nogueira's promises only spurred me on. That these hidden intentions were ridiculous, I knew well enough; but my dream swelled, unfolded, urged me on, crushing any resistance. I began to fear this vortex which, in the beginning, I had taken care should not be more than a diversion. It was, after all, like a cancer in my living tissue. Like a sick man who has tasted the death which awaits him, I suddenly began to think that *something had to happen*, and it was this sense of calamity which gave rise to the terror which

I was to lose only much later.

One day I looked at Nogueira and, not really thinking what I was doing and with my heart in my mouth, said to him: 'You've never been robbed, then?'

'Get away with you!' he replied.

'But what if someone did, one day?' I persisted.

'Who?'

'Me,' I replied.

'Come off it. Do you think I don't know who I'm working with?'

'That's all very well, but just suppose...'

'I don't want to suppose!'

'But it could well be.'

'Someone else in your place, maybe.'

'You've given me the keys, I deal with everything,' I said. Nogueira looked at me indulgently. 'I'd rather you kept the keys. I don't need them.'

'Are you afraid of losing them?'

'No, but...'

I immediately regretted my stupid outburst but Nogueira's faith in me seemed unshakable. This gave me a savage, ferocious elation, but at the same time I felt an endless terror. I wasn't interested in the future to the slightest degree. The thought of my son... but even this did not stop me.

Ideas came to me in flashes; I thought in images. I lived alternately in euphoria and terror. The balance of my will was brutally out of kilter. 'There is nothing to be done. Oh my God!' My hands shook. 'If this is going to be yours, let it be now, let it be now,' I thought. 'And why not? The old fool trusts you more and more.' – 'It can't be! It can't be!' The force of this other voice intimidated me, came to dominate me. I could no longer hear, without becoming restive, the hammering of the typewriter, the dry clatter endlessly repeated, and the sound of the little bell which seemed sometimes to suggest diabolical laughter, at others to whisper incitements.

In this soaring, vertiginous panic, my work became more of a muddle. I soon got angry. The need for lengthy periods of concentration exasperated me. My handwriting was all over the place, I needed an enormous effort of will just to hold my pen between my fingers; I got my numbers wrong, my sums, too. Between the moment that I saw an item and the moment that I entered it in the book, it changed as I wrote it, as if by magic or some conjuring trick. 'How did I make this mistake?' I asked myself. My mistakes distressed me. They made me think I was breaking down, becoming an automaton. (In fact I realised that this *force* was different from my will, and so I obeyed it.) I had dizzy spells, I ground my teeth, my sight clouded over, and for short periods I lost consciousness – only for it to begin again when I came round. My joints hurt, as if molten lead were burning them, and I seemed to need some outlet for this brutal force, to flex my muscles. I was frequently obliged to break off from my work. More than once I splintered my pen nib on the desk in a curt gesture of impatience. My chest felt oppressed, my breathing became laboured.

'It's only a bit of an injury,' I said, to justify my need for fresh air and movement. I went outside to give my head a rest, to fill my lungs with fresh air. I went down to the quays to see the boats leaving, the bustle which at other times had distracted me, trying to revive my old dream of voyages to far lands.

In vain: the idea had mercilessly wormed its way into my life. It no longer disappeared, as before, in the tumult of the streets. My life had become one of despair, listlessness and monotony. I became brutal.

'What's the matter with you? Are you ill?' asked Luisa one day, gazing horrified at the deepening shadows of my eyes.

'There's nothing wrong with me. Mind your own business!'

At about this time, like a ship whose rope has snapped and which drifts aimlessly, I began to cut myself off from her. Another love, abstract, incorporeal, which I couldn't resist, began to take the place of this placid affection – the love of a spectre which had arisen and was growing gradually in me. It was indeed a true love, a strange self-absorption, a delightful, repugnant intoxication, which burned up any feelings I had, just like those lovers who, divining our most hidden desires, satisfy them unto madness, exhaustion and death.

I only had enough energy left to love my son. Oh, how I carried on loving him, seeing in his pale flesh the palpable image of myself. I hated everything else, especially when it flew in the face of my plans.

I enjoyed seeing the office flourish; I liked to improve it, keep it looking good, modern, distribute some perfume through that room with its burden of foul thoughts and its musty smell. Whenever I went there I felt sad, cast down but at the same time in a fury. I just wanted to go to the safe, take out all the money and flee, in one fell swoop getting my hands on that which one day would be mine.

'But why? Why?' How had this, this diversion become this evil longing, this obsession, so that it possessed the very fibres of my being? 'It's too late now, my God!' I began to believe that there was no way out. How could I prevail in this mad, unequal struggle? 'I'm drowning, I'm being swept away by the current.'

Nogueira came in, red-faced, puffing and blowing, wiping his head; his eyes were smiling behind his shining spectacles – and I was no longer calm as before: rather, I felt a terrible bitterness. I had to clasp my hands together so as not to...

'No, not that, never!'

It was the logic of the *other one*.

I don't know how but I began to hate the old man. I thought that he had begun to be secretive in order to spy on me.

He would come now at different times. 'He wants to catch me at it.' But at what? Was there something I had forgotten to hide? Nevertheless, at certain times, seeing him come in I shook as if, in truth, he had caught me in the act.

I took measures to throw him off the scent. I mixed things up, there were anomalies in the books, mistakes intended to arouse his suspicions which I could then triumphantly show to be unfounded, thus renewing his faith in me.

I used to laugh to myself, a dismal, cruel laughter, reassured by the old man's naivety. Often, though, his blind faith exasperated me: 'Why does he not suspect anything? Why does he close his eyes, the fool?' But he didn't want to know. He just shook his head: 'Work it out in your own way. I'm sure it will come right.'

This dangerous game intoxicated me: I took it to the extremes of suspicion and recaptured his confidence almost by storm. Unfortunately he never understood that I was undermining this very confidence as part of my own defence.

'In the end I sorted out that mess that I told you about yesterday,' I explained to him in a forced way.

'All the better. Just as I told you!'

'But imagine if...'

'Leave it, leave it, there's nothing more to it.'

He went away; he didn't need explanations.

Many other times I craved his presence, gripped by an impulse that I could no longer resist. Oh, my life was like some barbaric torture that I endured with the courage of a stoic.

My hands, livid and cold, shook as I leafed through the

banknotes and cheques. 'He must not know. He must not...'

So that I wouldn't be alone I opened the dingy glass door and got to talking with the fellow worker on the other side. One day I noticed him looking at me in astonishment.

'Why are you looking at me like that?' I asked.

'Are you ill? Have you caught something?'

'What?'

'Your expression just now.'

'What's wrong with my expression?'

'I don't know; it just seems different, as if you'd changed.'

I looked at myself in the little mirror: I was unwilling to listen to him. 'Nonsense, there's nothing wrong with me,' I replied in a fury, suddenly appalled. I went to the door at the top of the steps, hesitating.

'Mr Renato.'

'Don't bother me any more!'

'Look, your hat...'

The boy, smiling, held it out to me, the hat I had left behind. Was he spying on me, too? Was he doing this to disconcert me? I looked at him in such a way that he stepped back. I went down the stairs, enraged, thinking: 'The kid has discovered my weakness and now he dares to play with me. And he knows nothing, nothing!' His blindness only made it twice as bad. The following day I couldn't look him straight in the face. His presence made me uncomfortable. He was a dangerous witness. I was afraid of him. Any excuse and I would get rid of him at once.

I wanted to run downtown to the money-changers where Nogueira spent his afternoons and shout at him: 'Can't you see that I am lost! Either send me away or have me arrested!'

Actions count for very little. Crime is the work of thought. And for thought there are neither bars nor prisons.

V I

The dreary life into which I have so easily slipped is beginning to get me down. Beyond my torment I feel the stirrings of revolt. Formerly my evenings were short and peaceful. As I read, in the silence of my house, by the lamp whose light Luisa was also using to sew, the only thing that broke the calm was the voice of our thoughts. Now they are a torrent which rages inside me, which roars and does not let me understand what I am reading. After forcing myself to read for a few minutes I close my eyes in despair. My eyes burn, the letters dance before them. Time passes so slowly, so insufferably slowly. I find no peace. What I have is no longer just a disease of the spirit: now I'm physically ill. I'm trying to fight against it.

What? Spend my evenings yawning or working to the bitter end, next to this woman who is always scared out of her wits? Life has a certain flavour, unmistakably its own, which has somehow filtered through to me; the thought astounds me.

Noise and laughter... In here no one laughs. My son is a sad creature, who could play all day with just a little straw, a trifling thing. My body needs a stimulus, something new. I want something different, a life of the senses which I have never had.

Here I am, a prisoner, like a train stuck on its tracks, the iron rails, endlessly. But no! I must leap clear even if, once off them, I roll down the hill right to the bottom of the abyss, like a derailed carriage.

I have become indifferent to Luisa. Sometimes I find even her presence intrusive. I have shut her out from my inner turmoil and my preoccupations. Her submissiveness irritates me, makes me uneasy. Now I go out every night, as I have never done before during our marriage. I go downtown, to the cafés – the drawing rooms of those who have neither rooms nor visitors – I wander around in the well-lit streets and squares, smoking. I derive an extraordinary satisfaction from this. How is it I have not discovered the city before? I used to find it perfectly normal to spend the evening at home, reading a book or a newspaper, going to bed early: it was even an adventure to go out before dinner. Now I keep relations to just a few words. I'm coming to believe that going out will cure me of what bedevils me. (What wouldn't I do to achieve that?)

I have entirely new horizons. I go to the cinema, the theatre; I'm astounded by my daring. I fix up an introduction to someone from the stage. A few days ago I found myself – I don't know how – in the dressing room of an actress in a revue so that I could give her my compliments.

So? These women in make-up – that's something new. It's as if I had never seen them. I stop and look around. I have new tastes. The images of those spent bodies, young, debauched, white... I begin to smile again.

I am happy. At this time my little boy, that chatterbox, is put to bed by his mother; she sighs and he asks, 'Daddy... Daddy?'

I manage to renew contact with some of my friends from my previous jobs, chaps who have gone up in the world, who have made something of themselves. There's a kind of satisfaction in meeting them again. I've changed! They've been leading quite different lives from me.

(So, what's conscience got to do with it anyway? How did I let all this pass me by without trying to latch onto it?)

When I leave the office I don't go straight home as I used to. In the middle of the drab rectitude of my life I have begun to taste the most fantastic attractions of pleasure, vice and

JOSÉ RODRIGUES MIGUÉIS

action. One night, after some gin and coffee, some of my friends succeed in dragging me off to a nightclub.

'Jazz?'

'What time is it?'

'Midnight.'

'Don't dither around!'

'Jazz... really,' I protest. 'I've never been anywhere like that. You're crazy. I...'

'Just for a look. You go in and straight out again.'

I let them take me. Half drunk, I find it impossible to resist. ('Have another one!') The gilded surroundings; I close my eyes and my body runs away – I'm flying through things, through space, out of time. Joy! Joy! What giddiness!

'The table's dancing!' I cry. 'The table's dancing! Put the light on!'

'It's crazy, he's crazy! Nobody's even switched the light off!' they say. 'Open your eyes.'

So many pairs of eyes are looking at me. I see the light of a fire. My God, the dawn is breaking; it looks like violets, violets in a green meadow. I'm going down to the bottom of the sea, seaweed all around, I'm floating... The light is golden now. My God, what sadness, this voice just doesn't stop! My hands, they're the hands of a dead person, they've lost all their strength. If only I could raise the glass to my mouth! My fingernails – they've turned purple!

'Don't get up. Just hold this, you!'

'I want... No. Who are they? I want to dance as well!'

I can hear them: 'He's crazy, now he wants to dance! He wants another glass. Don't let him.'

And the light; it's light, or is it raining forget-me-nots? The ash of my cigarette now is white, livid, insubstantial in the new, red light. The moon, what a moon! My hands are blue and my nails purple. It can't be, that's enough! What a band, sir! It's breaking my heart. Oh, how I want to laugh – and cry! The East: dancing girls, tents, minarets, the tawny sky, the exhausted bodies! I cry out. Now! Now I haven't even the strength to laugh. And then, in English, *'My heart is now waiting for you.'*

'Go easy!' someone says. 'You'll break it.'

The light is alive! The light is white!

'More, more, fill my glass!' I demand. 'This, this is what joy is, this is living, this fills my ears! "It's a long, long way to Tipperary..." What laughter, what joy! The ringing of glasses in time to the music. Take your hand away! Oh for some mad adventures! The sea! The sea! I'm on board ship... The music of skyscrapers! Look at the black man, that animal! Who is that fellow? Hey, black prince! Hey, buffoon! Look, he's flinging the baton away, the clown!'

I laugh madly, in a fit of crazy glee. I must do something for you. I laugh again. The champagne glass! My champagne glass – damn! I've broken it, it's there on the floor.

'You didn't see? Ha, ha!' I laugh. Nobody is going to notice what I do in the middle of all this confusion. 'How should I know if I'm talking too loud. Did I really throw the glass? Me, shouting?'

'Can't you shut up!' someone tells me. 'The fellow is mad!'

'Nobody saw it!' I shout. 'I don't want to know anyway! Go to hell.' I can't see anybody.

I'm laughing, laughing stupidly, horribly unkempt on my velvet seat. I'm in a terrible state. But it's good, it's so good to be released from my body. Ribbons of all colours wind themselves around me like snakes, the images are all distorted, they're hilarious. My movements are slow, fragmentary. My God, these jarring noises in my head. I put my head in my hands; as I close my eyes I begin to fall down the hillside at full pelt. Oh, what pleasure, what bliss, what bliss! And what terror. Catch me! Catch me! I'm going to fall, I'M FALLING! Ah!

JOSÉ RODRIGUES MIGUÉIS

I hear a voice: 'Come on, wake up there!'

Shapes, the light, colours – everything has changed.

What's going on? Two white arms around my neck. Oh let me graze those lips – so cool! – on your skin! How beautiful you are... (Can she hear me? I don't know) Your hands cool my brow and my eyes – just to close my eyes and skim my eyelashes against something so white and soft. Like that, like that. My face is burning, isn't it? Such cool, soft, peerless vertigo! Hold me! Hold me! Oh, how good I feel like this. Oh Lord, is it possible to be so happy! Hold me close, don't let me go, ever... Oh my God! I feel as though I'm falling to the bottom, falling, falling without end. (On your rounded breast, this mouth, biting.) Your dress, it's black velvet; you're not in mourning are you?

'No, don't fall asleep,' she prods me. 'You're falling asleep. We must go, you great lump!'

Your perfume. I don't know what words to use; they're in my head, but I can't speak clearly. How good it is! How good it is! (I'm so small, so very small.) Rolling easily, I'm flying. Crazy, me? What does it matter? I've drunk a bit too much... You lot can shut up, I'm not sleeping, I'm just happy – if only you knew how happy. Ah! Ah! And now, now? (If only they knew!) Hold me, hold me!

I'm slipping again, I can't stop myself, it's too quick – oh, what a shock that was!

'Get up!'

I obey and follow automatically, happy, as if I were someone else.

'She...' (I can't remember any more.)

My legs have gone. As if sleepwalking I slip on the polished parquet floor; they hold me securely in their arms. Everybody is looking at me. I can see them smiling. What a good feeling to be lifted like this, effortlessly. Is this my body? I laugh ('On your feet!'), I laugh in wild abandon, an irrepressible laugh, super-human, doleful, which deep down saddens me.

What time could it be? Time has ceased to exist. I'm going...

In the dawn, more sober, slipping into bed with my body still swaying, pounded by the barbaric rhythms of the jazz – how wonderful, the silence in this house – I understand how odious is this life of mine, always the same, alongside this woman who doesn't give a damn for me or my body. This wife of mine, who never utters a word of protest, gets on my nerves in the end. She doesn't even ask why I'm spending so much, or about the confetti and the bits of ribbon sticking to my jacket and shirtfront. My dumb anger flares up at the sight of her, docile and resigned, and her eyes, bruised with weeping and continuous lack of sleep – eyes full of pitiful, mute questioning. I'd rather she asked me straight out. (Images of last night flit across the mind's eye.) It intimidates me. I don't want to have to explain my actions to anyone. And if she starts weeping, I'm quite capable of hitting her. I'm sick and tired of being a slave. But she says nothing to me. Those other women, at least, don't want to know about our life. They're young, they're different. What do I care about weariness and wantonness? They're interesting, that's what matters!

I don't have to give excuses, or the slightest reason.

'Good night.'

It's morning, by the way. And I fall deeply asleep.

VII

I'm late into the office. The clerk is waiting for me, hunched up against the doorpost. Yes, my kidneys ache a bit, but a new life is coursing through my veins, my nerves, under my skin. I rejoice in the sunshine again. My colour seems better. My obsession is perceptibly waning. My work is more accurate. Perhaps I'll soon be free of this burden. I'm a different person, there's no doubt about it.

I'm not going to the club again tonight. I leaf through a magazine in the café, surprisingly self-assured. I'm full of pleasing ideas, hopeful plans. I'd like to start writing something. I get home early without having written a word. It will have to be another day.

'What say we go to the Bristol?' they suggest.

'What, again?' I ask.

'You made quite an impression.'

'You'll see today...'

'You don't remember all that,' I say, 'do you?'

'Oh, it was quite amazing.'

'And him there, with the champagne glass...'

'You haven't ever been to see her?' they ask.

'See who?' I ask.

'Mona Rubia.'

'Never.'

'So we've got to take him along...'

'No,' I reply, 'I'd rather have a beer. If you could see what...'

'She's something special. She's got the most beautiful legs you've ever...' (Clapping.) 'And she's only twenty, by god!'

I'm lost in the laughter, in the swirl of a thousand conversations; it's impossible to talk to anyone properly. Snatches of words, phrases, all disconnected. This is the kind of thing I need so much! Laughing, I protest – but I no longer try very hard to resist temptation. I'm going back; I'll always go back. I can't stop laughing. It's the purest, most instinctive feeling of enjoyment. In a mirror I can see a new brightness in my eyes, colour in my cheeks... I've changed, I'm completely different. I like it like this.

These days I'm always late at the office. Since the clerk has to be in on time I give him the key. Every night I meet up with these friends of mine. Most of them work, like me; they're decent chaps. They just want to have fun; that's natural enough, isn't it? Nogueira goes back home early so there's no danger of him knowing where I spend my evenings. If he comes in specifically for something I never fail to tell him about 'the evenings I work late'.

Time, like a great, silent, smooth ball, rolls by without much happening.

I open and empty the desk without blinking. My papers fly about, all mixed up. I give vent to my madness in a dry bark of laughter. Anyone who has had a childhood like mine has got to get even sometime, hasn't he? That's why I'm doing this. Besides, the business is doing well. The combination of Nogueira's foresight and everything I've done for him has put this place in an enviable position. I'm not having anyone to help with the book-keeping; my pretext is that I can manage everything myself. But in fact these days I'm farming out some of the work to an old friend of mine.

I love the cinema because it feeds my sense of fantasy. That solitary, silent pleasure, in that room full of people lost in the shadows, gives me a real kind of interior richness that I need so much. It's as if some films embody my own thoughts and bring them to life, up there on the screen.

Meanwhile my circle of acquaintances is improving. I get myself a better wardrobe, pay attention to my appearance; I

JOSÉ RODRIGUES MIGUÉIS

get to know women and even their brief embrace is, when all is said and done, worth at least a month of married life. I don't feel tired. Over this period I put on weight. In the end taking my pleasure is just a physical exercise like any other; it calms one down and of course I pay generously. It was what I had been needing all along.

It's a beautiful Sunday and Nogueira turns up in my house, very early. I'm annoyed – what with me still in bed, unshaven, and Luisa hastily trying to bath our son. He's got a box of cakes for the boy and a length of cloth for Luisa to make something from. He sits the boy in his lap and bounces him up and down on his knees, galloping like a horse, then hoists him into the air, kissing him, all the while beaming, red-faced and telling stories of the Brazilian prairies. He makes a wonderful grandfather, so tender is he. Smiling sadly, Luisa observes him appreciatively.

'Say Grandpa, say Grandpa,' he urges.

'Oh, Mr Nogueira,' says Luisa.

From the corner I look on, gloomily. The old fool seems to want to get close, to become part of the family. It gets on my nerves that he should want to pass as the boy's grandfather. (Luisa has never known her parents.) As he leaves he slips fifty escudos into the boy's hand and promises to return. The boy thinks he's wonderful and Luisa finds him very congenial.

'Who knows,' she says after he has left. 'Perhaps for the little one he could be a guardian angel, a kind of grandfather. Why don't we have him round one day?'

I shrug by way of response: 'Don't be so foolish; mind your own business and leave me to look after the kid's future. That's what I'm here for.'

'Your wife seems a bit down,' he says to me the following day. 'Is she anaemic? A few days in the country would do her good.'

Happy Easter   55

This kindly interest puts me on the defensive.

He's not going to get involved in my life, he might hear something. I'm going to keep an eye on him.

When I get home it's already dawn; I'm burned out by these pleasures which I'm beginning to find disgusting and all the same. Going straight to my room I take off my shoes, my jacket, loosen my collar which is choking me, and begin to listen to my son's breathing. I pull back the curtain of his cot: he's sleeping on his side, his golden curls against the whiteness of his pillow, his right hand under his cheek, his left arm flung out with his fist clutching tightly those tiny, invisible treasures. His iron bedstead rocks gently to the rhythm of his breathing.

'And to think that he will be a man one day.'

I am seized by a terrible anxiety for the future which I am preparing for him. I am amazed, almost frightened, by his grace, his colour, all so different from me as a child and from the mother who carried him in her belly. I feel both proud and jealous. He's blond like the mother he resembles. In vain do I look in his face for any sign, any token of me. His little nose, straight though not yet shaped, is graceful and fresh; his ears are pink and tiny, perfect as jewels. His light eyes are pure, calm and deep; the silken eyelids which cover them are fringed with thick, long, blond lashes. I long to cover his mouth with kisses – his little red mouth, with its two symmetrical little curves disappearing into two tiny dimples. Puckered up it seems to be searching for the breast or sketching a kiss. This fragrant little life, I was the one who begat it. I look at him and the ideas dance around in my head.

'It's you that I am plundering,' I think to myself.

His little head seems to me to have a halo of distant light – a star which I observe from the bottom of the abyss. My brow furrows and I feel my veins swell under my unruly thatch of hair, much of which has already turned white. I slide his tiny

JOSÉ RODRIGUES MIGUÉIS

arm under the sheet and, stifling a sigh, carry on to bed.

She pretends to be asleep so as not to trouble me; her body has left me plenty of room in the bed. I can sense her there quite clearly, the trembling of her body, her constricted breathing. Once again the anger and spite, the depravity and recklessness arise in me. An evil passion convulses me. In a murderous fit I clench my fists over her like a thief in the night.

I know well enough how malevolent and cruel I am. But I didn't know this shameful vileness when I saw you, unmarried, graceful, simple, so deserving of a faithful, unswerving love, there in your dark dress, your eyelids languidly, artlessly covering your eyes like two hidden violets. Did I really come to love you?

I lie down silently.

Every morning at breakfast my little boy sits on my lap. I leave with a sour taste in my mouth, after absent-mindedly kissing Luisa, who I can see is wasting away. From the window the little fellow shouts out lovingly, little things, blowing me kisses and bringing tears to my eyes. 'Bye-bye Daddy, bye-bye Daddy,' he calls.

His little voice, laughing, sounds on high in the clear morning sun like the chirping of a bird which casts its song into space. Between the bars I can see him talking with his mother, kicking stones with his little feet, pointing at something and laughing. I turn to say goodbye at the corner (if I forget to do it he'll let me know about it in the evening) and when I get on the tram I fall back into the absurd monotony of my days. I feel that my nerves, wearied by pleasure, demand rest and peace.

The end of the year is drawing near.

Nogueira has gone at last to Brazil to sell up his business there. He left and I was alone to cope with things, with my beastly life – nights on the town, women, dinners, gambling.

The staff of the late-night restaurants, the clubs, the casinos around the capital all know my generosity and bow, smiling to greet me. Before closing the balance of the year just ended I collect my share of the profits, a share which Nogueira has once more increased.

'We'll close for four or five days,' I say to the clerk. 'Come in and pick up the mail, see if there's anything needs doing urgently and sit on it until I return.'

'Where are you going?' Luisa asks me in surprise.

'On a business trip,' I reply.

'At this time of year? What about the office?'

'It's nothing to do with you,' I retort.

'Write to me,' she begs.

'Maybe,' I say, 'if I have time, of course.'

Six days. In a whirlwind of six days I squander everything I've saved during the year. I travel through Andalucia by car, accompanied by women and friends. It is the last flaring of a great conflagration.

On a cold, cloudy January day my rage explodes. I have returned drained and penniless. The accounts are a complete shambles, as though a madman's hand or a witch's art have jumbled everything up.

'How could it have been me who did all this?' I ask myself. But it was I who had done it.

And now my eyes can see; there is no point in disputing the clear import of the facts. Feeling an unbearable bitterness, I want just to close my eyes, to sleep or to die.

The mere presence of this clerk could be disastrous; I'll find some excuse to boot him out and take on some other young fellow.

My weariness is unbounded and I'm losing my appetite for the sort of adventures I've had lately. I'm growing to hate those whose company I favoured, I avoid their persistent visits and cease to search them out.

How much do I owe? I can't begin to work it out. I pay up with a terrible calmness. Of course me creditors are robbing me, but I daren't, I can't, question anything. I just pay up – or rather, Nogueira's coffers do.

The days pass, gloomily, slowly.

The old man is just back from Brazil and his presence reminds me of the state I'm in. 'I don't want to know about it,' I keep telling myself. I feel only disgust with life, I can't think straight, I just shrug my shoulders. If some sudden happening doesn't galvanise me into action I'll just be swallowed up little by little in these quicksands.

Treacherously, almost without my realising it, my hidden resolve has overcome me. It is forcing me to see clearly my ruin – my son's plight – but not even that gives me the resolve to save myself. The other one, the one who inspired and guided me, tells me what to do instead: I have to falsify the balance, the bills of deposit in the banks. Nogueira laughs, satisfied with the year's results. He slaps me heartily on the back and slips a platinum ring, with a fine Brazilian diamond, onto my finger. I thank him for the keepsake, but two days later I secretly sell the ring.

'Why aren't you wearing the ring I gave you?' he asks.

'Oh, you know, I'm not used to wearing valuable jewellery,' I reply. 'I've put it in the bank.'

His Brazilian business has been wound up. For whole days on end I listen wearily to all the details. Nogueira has decided to buy the farm of his dreams and entrusts the money to me.

What if he should go to the bank and find out that I've been cooking the books? To avoid I don't know what disgrace I rush to deposit this huge sum of money. An invisible cord is choking me. But no; he's often in the Rua do Comércio – to see his brokers, or a friend who's a moneychanger – but he never sets foot inside the bank.

Life like this is unbearable. I can't move; I'm someone in rehabilitation therapy who has lost the very idea of certain movements and has to learn everything anew. Just the slightest noise makes me jump. 'Come on, calm down,' I tell myself – but I can't.

Tenderness and joy, suffering and love, everything which is part of the past, my past, is buried beneath all this ignominy. There's only one thing which lingers, remaining in me like the chaste, musical murmuring of a trickle of water which will not dry up in the most parched summer: the love of my son. This is what keeps me going – keeps me working, and keeps me at home, with my insipid wife, whose submissiveness fills me with disgust.

A son... After its first curiosity has been satisfied, love loses its passion and its appeal, and becomes just a vague sort of tenderness which in turn is snuffed out, leaving only toil. The woman was soul and body, then just body, which finally became useless and heavy. The soul, anxious for creation, left her with the first son. Yes, that one. He is the flesh of my flesh, the continuation of my life, the inspiring and mysterious promise of immortality. A son is a step in life beyond us, a piece of the future that we create and launch into the unknown. The light that the stars, long since dead, still cast into the ether.

JOSÉ RODRIGUES MIGUÉIS

VIII

I get home in time for dinner; it's Friday. My son doesn't come to the door. 'The little one, how is he?' I ask, as usual.

Luisa says nothing; her eyes are red and swollen.

'Answer me, you fool. How is the boy?' I say, shaking her violently.

'He's ill in bed...'

'What are you saying?'

She begins to sob with such force that I go pale with fear. She holds onto me weeping uncontrollably; her pent-up sorrow needs to be shared with another but I thrust her from me almost brutally. 'Let me go, you fool. Why are you crying?'

I can't stand displays of feeling like this; tears infuriate me, they fill me with foreboding. I storm into his room: on the uncovered bed my son is sleeping on his back; he is very red and his eyes are closed. His clenched hands are resting on the outer fold of the sheet, which is startlingly white. Trembling, I bend over him: his breathing is slow and laboured. As usual I place his soft little arms under the sheets and put my hand on his forehead: it is burning. He groans, almost inaudibly, without opening his eyes. Will he call out for me? I am stricken by terror and weakness; my legs feel weak. 'He's very ill, he's very ill,' I cry.

Sweat pours down my brow and I ask Luisa, who has silently followed me: 'But how has this happened? The doctor, have you called one? What did he say? Speak softly...'

My eyes never leave her. Standing in the door, her voice quavering with suppressed sobs she tells me that the little one has been ill for two days. He has refused to eat, cried all the time and complained that his head and throat were sore.

'I didn't tell you earlier so as not to upset you; I thought it would soon be over,' she says. 'I can't tell you anything; you're never around long enough.'

I grab her by her thin wrist and I can feel her trembling. I don't know what to say to her; it is as if I have a huge knot in my throat. I can see that she too is making a huge effort to speak and so I wait for her. Her voice has a strange quality; somehow it reminds me of damp violets. 'I could see he was very ill,' she says. 'Then he became drowsy and I called the neighbour on this side and asked her to go and get the doctor. I don't even know how I had the courage to stay here alone with him.'

I hardly touch my simple dinner. I can hear Luisa sighing, looking at me anxiously, in a silent question. Neither of us ventured anything. 'You're not eating anything then?' I ask. 'I can't even look at it,' she replies. 'I'm worried to death.'

I spend the night sitting beside him; I fight back my rising groans. It was him I had been needing. I can see him with his little hands crossed in the coffin. I get up abruptly. He's alive – but the picture comes back again and again, time without number. I can hear him breathing; his breath rasps in his throat. The night-light throws red, dancing glimmers on the walls. The atmosphere is heavy with anxiety and expectation. I think he moved; but no, it was the fluctuating shadows. I can see spectres on the smooth walls; I cover my eyes with my hands so as not to see them. From time to time the little boy murmurs something I can't make out. I bend over him to try to hear. There's no doubt he's delirious.

'What about the doctor, isn't he coming?' I ask.

The pain is hammering at my chest, my temples. Will he be the one who will pay for my wrongdoing?

'Why can't it be me?' I cry.

'What are you saying?'

JOSÉ RODRIGUES MIGUÉIS

'Ah, you're there, are you?' I ask. She doesn't reply.

In despair I think: 'I'd rather he died. What? I must be crazy! How could that be! He must live, I demand that he live, my son. I demand it! My darling, my beautiful son...'

'What's the matter? Are you crying? Don't cry.'

'Let me be. Leave me to my...' My tears don't let me finish.

At last the doctor arrives. He's a decent old fellow with a big white beard and glasses. His manner, his very presence calms us. He seems to take an age to examine the sick little boy. In what a leisurely fashion he washes his hands! I hand him a linen towel, edged with lace, and he unfolds it with such care. Luisa has fled, so as not to hear him. Anguished, I gaze at him: 'Well then, Doctor?'

'We'll see. For the moment I'm not going to offer a firm diagnosis. I don't like the look of his throat at all. His breathing is difficult. I'll be back tomorrow morning. Try to help your wife get better, too; she's very weak, a bag of nerves. She needs a sedative, I'll give you a prescription.'

He sits down at the desk of our bedroom and silently begins to write, in tiny, illegible handwriting, taking care over the words. I think I'm going to faint. Somewhere a clock is ticking – a heartbreaking sound which seems to flit across the bedroom.

'About the little one...'

'Yes, what?' I reply.

'You must move him to another room as soon as possible; he needs more air and sun. Then we shall see. And this is for your wife – a teaspoonful with every meal. Disinfect the sheets. For his hands...' Thus he gives us our instructions, so calmly, and puts his pen back in his pocket, as well as something shiny, a tube of glass or metal.

'I hope all will be well with you,' he says.

'I understand a bit better now, doctor,' I reply, trying to smile, although my head is spinning. I run back to the room

Happy Easter 63

to look at my son; he's even redder, burning with fever. I'm scared stiff. Suppose we call another doctor?

I try to comfort Luisa as best I can.

She makes up his little bed in a room at the front which catches the early sun. There, where was once a sitting room, is now the nest of this sick little creature. The walls, a kind of burnt pink, are cheering – they give us some hope.

I doze, fearful, obsessed by a nameless longing. Morning comes and, overcome by sorrow, it seems that I am less contemptuous of this decent, long-suffering woman; full of bitter pity I gaze at her eyes which are as sad as a winter dawn. I kiss them; they are two dewy little flowers. 'Be brave, girl,' I whisper.

It is the first sign of tenderness since my fall. I go down the stairs and suddenly something powerful seems to grip my throat and I burst forth into tears again. Oh my God, I can still cry, I still have feelings, I still have a heart.

Out of habit I look up from the street at the closed windows. I see her silhouette in the window where the curtains are drawn back; she has a white handkerchief. I say goodbye to her. I feel an immense sorrow, for her and for me, as well as remorse, fear and foreboding. My exile will now be all the more unbearable. Coward!

I can no longer walk the streets at night. I see him every-where, choking, his little hands reaching out to me. Fear binds me to his iron cot. In his room there is a pervasive smell of medicines and disinfectant.

Nogueira, I suppose, will continue to demonstrate his blind faith in me, but I have no more faith in myself and, what is worse, I cannot rest for a single moment. Every day I see more clearly what I have done, weighing the harm I have caused. There's nothing I can do to put it right. I work without saying a word, my heart beating furiously. I don't know how I can carry on.

JOSÉ RODRIGUES MIGUÉIS

There's nothing for it but to sell our new furniture. With silent amazement Luisa watches it all disappear. She doesn't protest and I don't dare offer any explanation: 'It has to be done, it has to be done. There's nothing more to say. You know how bad business has been – and it's getting worse, worse.'

IX

There, at home, I spend the long evenings as this rainy winter draws to an end: throughout the night I listen to the wind as it rattles the windows, and the rain as it beats ceaselessly on the panes. In this street the noises die down early. I am alone on the silent fourth floor while she rests after a long day's toil. From time to time, though, she opens the door; she peeps in at me and I can see her in the dark, her eyes sad and lifeless in her pallid face, the dark mop of her hair hanging loose. She doesn't say a word. I motion to her to go to bed, the door closes and the silence resumes. But within me a kind of indefinable questioning never stops; I feel the sobs rising in my throat, a sea of tears that I can't seem to release.

Life has come to seem a futile torment, lacking either beauty or grandeur, in which the cost of a moment's pleasure is long years of bitterness.

I work as never before. I want to save my son, so that I leave him neither debts nor difficulties. I know just how harsh men can be where honour is concerned – at least towards the beaten and the disgraced. And if I fail him, God knows!

I have taken on work at home and long into the night I hear only the scratching of my pen on the smooth paper, and the canary in the dining room, startled by the light, sharpening its beak on its perch. It cheeps timidly. Could it be some question I can't understand, a friend's advice?

What are such useless creatures doing on this earth? This thing's destiny is just to eat and sing. But there are others who suffer like me although they are not answerable for the harm they do. I suffer – and it sings! It isn't free; but then what would become of it without our protection, out of the golden cage where it wants for nothing? (Love itself is a struggle to the death.) Fine, I am free: but an invisible chain binds me to my suffering. I am a prisoner of my own freedom! What is freedom but the right to bear pain heroically – without blaming anyone else for it? I can hardly bear to hear it sing. The contrast infuriates me. Supposing I set it free? No, it would be better to kill it. I need to see some blood spilt, my grief needs some outlet. One night, in exasperation, beside myself, I open the dining room door. (The thing is quiet for once, perhaps sensing the danger.) A moment is enough, and I can understand the blind urge for revenge, the need to defy one's fate, which goads me to kill it. Ah, but Luisa, she cares for it so much! No, I'd better let it live.

This episode though only heightens the contrasts in my life. In the end I get used to listening to it, and once more my work becomes the drug which sets me free, allowing me to dream of release from my responsibilities.

The process of death unfolds before my eyes, even to the final decomposition of the body, in diabolical, perverse clarity. A shiver... I throw myself into my sums in despair, in a painful hurry to get somewhere, though where I don't know. Oh, I do believe in the remission of my sins through sacrifice; perhaps I can even save myself. When all is said and done there are in me, as in everybody, several persons; and these persons are so incompatible that one of them must prevail at a given time as far as my actions are concerned. It's some sort of religious feeling, no doubt, this appeal to 'something higher'.

I add up, count, write, divide, in a fever. The numbers dance in the air before me, blown in flurries of hallucination. How can I work like this? I can't think, I can't even calculate. It's as if someone is whispering to me the results of calculations that I haven't made; my work is mechanical and swift. The exercise books with their ruled pages pile up, full of my nervous handwriting. Who is guiding my mind's work, my arm's movements? One night I rouse myself to confront the shadows which drive me on – but, damn, there's nobody there.

It's a delirium. Every time my haste is greater. I feel that I am slipping into madness. I feel the breath of hallucination on my skin and then it is gone. I know there is a dark abyss beneath me, but I still carry on. Like a student waiting for his examinations I chew the fingernails of my left hand. My back and my arm ache from being bent so long over my writing.

To save my son I will need to repay everything, but his medical expenses are costing me every penny I have. My pen creeps over the paper, squeaking, in a deathly, nervous haste. Its doleful scratching seems to spread like a veil, opened out, wafting here and there through the house, this almost empty house, and so much bigger now that I have had to sell the furniture.

I spend nights on end without sleeping. In my few hours of rest I toss and turn, stifling my sighs, as a thousand and one forebodings and evil thoughts swarm through my mind with a noise like the roar of a waterfall. And it's there, above all, in that dark bedroom, that those phantoms spring forth. The agony goes on and on, until the break of day.

'What's the matter?' asks the resigned voice at my side.

'Nothing,' I reply. 'Go back to sleep.' I hear her sigh and we carry on, both of us spinning out this sleepless night.

I am beginning to need her company. Little by little I am beginning to feel a grievous, infinite pity for this woman, who watches over my life. I spare her a fleeting caress, I hold her trembling hand, clammy with sweat. Now I can see this decent, modest woman, who has sacrificed so much, suddenly alone, so timorous and weak, with her little boy in her arms. I see her, and I struggle in vain against the fear that I might have to leave these two poor wretches. Dying is the least of my worries. I have to save them, make up for the immense harm I've done them (and Nogueira, too, that kind man with his gentle words), even if I then have to die, for at least some peace and contentment will be restored to the house.

Nobody could possibly imagine what now drives me on, this idea upon which my whole life has focused.

At daybreak, when the hand of light knocks discreetly on the windowpane, she gets up silently to close all the doors in the house so that the sun won't disturb me. She doesn't come back to bed. Though I am grateful to her I can't open my mouth to thank her.

I'm starting to love her again, but it's a love which comes from a longing for what we have and for what we have given up. How can I put it? It is a love born of repentance and regret. In the white vessel of her body – I can't think of touching it – I see my long gone past, irredeemable, irrecoverable. And I love her as she was – or, rather, as I wished she had been – the past that never was, the one I should have had.

Her labours, to which the short night barely gives surcease, begin early. At dawn, worn out by my ceaseless stream of thoughts, I slip into a dull drowsiness almost before I know it; it is a mixture of sleep, exhaustion and torpor. While I doze I can hear the cautious steps of her thickly stockinged feet. Then the door to the stairs opens, a sigh of relief as she goes off in the dawn light to buy a few things. Through the thin veil of my sleep I recall now distant feelings. What? I recognise that voice speaking to me, that rainy day: 'Where I come from there used to be...' The memory of bitter words, of injustices, fills me with anguish and remorse. That first day at school, how lonely I felt, my tears, that little

70   JOSÉ RODRIGUES MIGUÉIS

bundle of food for my snack.

My father: I can see him, dead – who would have thought it? – with his thin, discoloured hands clasping a wooden cross, the blood-stained cloth round his head... this image which I thought I had forgotten terrifies me. And what is this yellow light? Sheets of paper inlaid with gold and black, the noise of sobbing and sighing. On the black velvet, tears glisten like stars and I stretch out my finger to touch them. 'No, don't!' I try to force myself to think of something pleasant. It's unbearable. And now a letter. 'No, not this either.' That dark green coat, my mother's, that we had to sell one day – the bread had run out. 'I don't want to. I don't want to.' And then suddenly a cross blots out the other images; how can this be? I cry out to what good there may have been in my past; a feeling of remorse or longing, a kiss. What happened to her? Is she dead too? A flat field – and crosses. My eyes, shut tight, are swollen with tears which trickle down my cheeks and splash onto the pillow.

'Look at the time!'

'Where are you going,' she asks. 'You're not going out, are you?'

'Yes,' I reply, 'I've got to go.'

'It's four o'clock. What on earth are you going to do out there?'

'I've told you. I've got to go.'

'It's pouring down,' she says.

'What the devil does it matter?'

'Oh my God,' she cries.

'Let me go, let me go,' I say, 'I'm in a hurry, can't you see?'

'But what is it you want? Are you ill?' asks my wife.

She tries to hold on to me. I have to go. I jump out of bed, put on my trousers and shoes in haste. My hands are shaking, I can't do up my buttons. 'Don't say anything. Don't ask me anything.'

I turn up my collar and leave, closing my ears to Luisa's pleading. Where am I going? My resolve is as firm as it is idiotic. Something is calling me which brooks no refusal. The streets are deserted and running with rain. I hear only my footsteps which echo against the walls of the houses. I quicken my steps; it's cold and my teeth chatter. This house... I stop in front of it; I don't know it. I don't really know where I am; everything is dark. I touch the stones, doors, and go in. Is it I who am walking, or is it these things which are moving and changing all around me? Rooms, huge rooms, all of them cold, shadowy and deserted; an abandoned house. I don't know where I am going but some force, which I follow, is driving me on. Before me there is an immense, black iron door. I look at it, touch it: it reaches to the ceiling and it feels cold, so cold. My teeth chatter like castanets. My frozen fingers hurt but with all my strength I struggle to open it. It's so heavy. It opens, silently. A safe? Yes, a safe, so dark it seems like a cave. I'm fearful but I plunge into it, feeling my way and exploring its shadowy depths where there is a slight glimmer of stones and metal. And then I see, I see! The safe is crammed with riches, I can't believe it, they're mine, they're all for me. My senses are drunk with the opulence of knowing they're mine. I bury my hands, shaking and livid in the unnatural phosphorescence of the gems, in the gold and the precious stones, which fall softly through my fingers.

In haste I cram into my pockets as many stones as they can hold: there's no way of taking all of them. I'm drunk, a delicious, voluptuous warmth runs through my body, into my hands, and then everything around me starts to dance, the gemstones jump, spin and whirl and glitter.

I cry aloud 'It's all mine, it's all mine!' Then there is a rumble, dull and menacing; everything disappears, the gems vanish like snuffed out candles. 'The door! Open the door!' Someone has locked me in the safe. 'Open the door, the door!'

I bang on it desperately. But now there is nothing, no walls, nor door, nor gemstones. 'Open up! Open up!' I can hear the creaking of chains. I'm going to die in here. 'The door!' I'm suffocating. 'Air!'

I'm in agony, soaked through with sweat.

I can no longer sleep: this dream has driven away sleep. I heave myself up and sit watching the dawn break outside the window, in the sad grey silence of this winter morning. A wan, sullen light spreads across the fronts of the houses as they emerge gradually from the shadowy chaos of the night. Shapes, colours; the branches of the bare trees shake and the last drops of rain run down the window-panes like silent tears.

I have begun to hate my bed, and now I can't fall asleep with any ease of mind. I wake up with a start, my mouth open and dry, feeling that I'm falling headlong. A terror that I can't control convulses my body and the bed as well, and I lie awake for long hours, observing with morbid interest the slow restoration of calm to my body. At the foot of our bed – we're back in our modest bridal bed – a loose bit of metal rattles, like ironic laughter, in time with the beat of my heart. I push the bedclothes against it to muffle the unwelcome sound. I plead with the mysterious powers of night to let me rest from my struggle, just for a few hours. Now I pray fervently – I don't know why, since I no longer believe in God and I have forgotten all the prayers I ever learned.

I know some of my nightmares as well as if they were books read again and again. They come back, with the same anguish and the same intensity and hidden force. It's useless for me to keep telling myself – in that part of me which is always awake – that it is all just a brief illusion. I have to go through this test; I yield to the absurd as to my unavoidable fate.

My unease knows no bounds. (And still this dread of

parting pulses through me.) Everything is deserted, the quay, the boat; the atmosphere is strangely supernatural. It is the very moment of departure. There are no shouts, no noises on the quay nor on board. It is a phantom boat, fluid, insubstantial. (I am dreaming of course, but it's good for me to dream like this.) Silently it drifts away from the land, which is hidden in a dense mist. We set sail for the open sea. Everything is so quick, so light. The air is stifling. Not even the call of a bird can be heard, nor any human voice. The ship ploughs the waves. A raging wind springs up without warning and a dense, continuous rain is falling. It's beautiful to watch the rain on the sea. Everything is grey – the sky, the great waves, the boat, me too. Only a sliver of orange light, becoming gradually and almost imperceptibly paler, until it is a wan shade of green, pierces the horizon. I can't escape the infinite sadness of this detail – a sigh of light from Beyond which cuts this sky and lies along the waves. Night falls, sudden and opaque, over the phosphorescent sea. My apprehension returns; on the crests of the unrelenting waves the foam boils furiously. Nobody! Nobody! Not a cry. I am alone. It's a long time since I scoured the ship in all directions, stumbling, slipping, holding on to the ropes, the gunwales, to things I don't know, can't make out, in the silence and the mist. There's not a soul to be seen. Suddenly in the darkness the ship is transformed and I find myself in a small boat, cast off, without oars or a sail, as if in a coffin. I have been shipwrecked. I've been fighting the sea for hours. The boat is shipping water. I bail out furiously but the water rises inexorably, mocking my useless efforts. Exhausted, I stretch myself out, turning my face to the sky, a face damp with tears and the salt drops of the sea. I sob and, wavering, pray to some unknown God. I slip towards the cold, unremitting waves. I dive, I float on the water, I cry, I flap my arms desperately, my hair plastered against my eyes; above me I dimly

JOSÉ RODRIGUES MIGUÉIS

imagine the smooth, fateful flight of the birds. How long have I been like this? The waves sweep me towards a looming coastline, the cliffs sheer, where the waves break in towering spray. In the depths of the night the waves pound relentlessly on the shore, the howling, ghostly white spume like a shroud. The waves drive me on, irresistibly. I let go, drained of all strength. A few yards away the storm rages on. The waves smash against the rocks with a noise like thunder.

Death, death in the raging foam! The crows with their iron beaks skim my flesh. A bigger wave lifts me now, ready to smash me against the sharp ridge of the quay, tearing me into bloody tatters. And the crows!

An immense cry (I am caught in the encircling spume) bursts from me, perhaps from the storm itself. I reach out and clench my hands, to hold myself up, to combat the force which is sweeping me along...

Panting, delirious, groaning, sobbing, in my distress I grab the crumpled bedclothes. Pityingly, her hands ease my pain, they smooth my dishevelled hair, caress my clammy forehead, which is already lined and aged. From her mouth pour soothing, gentle maternal words which remind me of my mother, dead now for so long.

I hold her and cry: 'My love, where would I be without you?'

I weep; and then, calm at last, I kiss her with tender humility and gratitude.

X

At my side her white, submissive body is always waiting. I hardly dare touch her; is it superstition or diffidence? I'm fearful of opening a new chapter of tenderness and of sad sensuality. I have only ever offered a rare, fleeting caress to this sweet body which at first intoxicated me, before I came to hate it. Neither of us can bring ourselves to believe in sexual pleasure, although I know that it offers me the only legitimate delight which remains in my bitter, ruined life. I don't have the courage to make the first move, though I know she wants it too – in silence, or in the chaste murmur of spring water.

Is it right to be constantly subduing the flesh in this way and to find exaltation only in pain? Haven't we a right to something more in our lives? In her world there is neither joy nor sunlight. Shouldn't I show some love to this poor, downtrodden, suffering woman whom I have made so unhappy? Perhaps some pure instinct, born of redemption, stops me from holding her tight in my arms as I did before. Once again, with all my being, I want the fresh, virginal woman I first kissed. I remember our old love, so pure and intense, those nights which passed so quickly while our bodies burned in sensual rapture and the dawn found us sleeping in each other's arms. Only later did the presence of our son fill us with shame.

And now, with him ill, there in his little white bed in the small room off ours... No, no, it would be a sacrilege to take her in my arms. Our pleasure would be no more than a lament above the abyss, and our frenzy merely end in tears of shame.

I'm living as much in the midst of a nightmare as in reality itself. Just like the survivors of a fire or a shipwreck who are forever haunted by the horror of that tragedy, I live under the spell of fear. In broad daylight, there in the street, the images won't let me go. I have a terrible fear that I'm going completely mad. If anyone were to see me in this state running down the street, my head bursting, he would certainly stop to look at me and assume that I was on the run from the madhouse or prison.

Only Luisa's company can keep my fear within bounds. Just to know that she is there to assuage my suffering is enough to give me some peace. For a few nights I manage to sleep peacefully and I begin to think I am almost better. Tonight, after some particularly exhausting work, I go to bed in silence, overwhelmed by things as usual, but soon I fall into deep sleep, a rare thing indeed.

Then, suddenly: 'What? It's impossible!' I cry. I am travelling across a broad street, lit by a warm spring sun. I'm light-hearted like the air around me; my joy is pure and unforced: I'm amazed to feel so secure and full of well-being. But how can this be? I thought I had gone to bed late, deadly cold, worn out. So how can I be in *this* street, in the morning sun, and so happy? No, no, this sense of assurance, of my life being safe, it's all a lie, it's all just a dream.

I am forcing myself to see clearly. I am trying to see *myself as if I were someone else*, as happens so often when we dream. But it's in vain; some force compels me to accept the reality. 'But I've only just gone to sleep in my own bed.' And I don't know where I am, nor where I'm going. I can't explain it, however much I keep telling myself that I am asleep. It's so long since I felt such a wholesome happiness, I give myself up to it. It's wonderful to live like this, however short the moment. Just to believe you're happy. What did I do that was so unusual? I'm walking on air, I'm so happy. And meanwhile – however odd it might seem – although I don't really know these bright, sunny, clean avenues, yet some part of me *does* recognise them. There's something unreal about them. I can't recall having seen them, but still I *feel* that I must know them. Is it a new city? I can't quite... Brazil. Brazil? yes, that's just it. Nogueira – Brazil, exactly. I understand, now I understand perfectly; I'm on my way to the office, in Brazil, in... Damn, never mind the name. What bliss. As I go along I can see the fronts of the fine houses, the rows of trees in blossom. Over everything there's something supernatural, a sort of scent, a foretaste of something. And the warm air, new, washed clean, the sky rejoicing (the feeling I had as a child on holy days.) The silence, the silence! In the empty streets the brightness smiles. Where is everybody? I suppose it's very early still. I breathe deeply and the air comforts me. How silent it all is!

Ah, now here they come. Round the corner comes the head of a procession. They linger; there are so many of them, men, only men, their heads bare and bowed. The crowd swells, packed close together. Not a cry, not a step is heard, as if they were walking with extreme care on a carpet. I too walk without making a noise; their silence overwhelms me. I open my eyes wide to see. There they go, overflowing round the corner and pouring into the street, slow, black, all of them. It's a continuous flow, constant; I see the regular movement of their bodies and the deadly silence stifles me in the light. Nobody even opens a window, it's horrible. Something strange is happening. Their grief, their anguish begins to afflict me, too. Bewildered, I press forward to see. They take no notice of me, they don't speak to me, not even when I try to make my way through the crowd which offers no bodily resistance. I tremble; can I be brushing against phantoms, passing through their midst, through bodies I can see but not touch, beyond the law of physics? Their figures are indistinct,

I can't make out their faces, and these are the heart of the procession: the men are slowly pulling a small, low carriage, it's virtually a handcart. Nobody looks at me. I have to see – no, it's not worth it – they're almost here.

'Excuse me, please.'

My curiosity is agonising: 'Didn't I say so? Didn't I say so?' I can see an enormous coffin, black and uncovered. 'I don't want to see, I must go.' My heart beats wildly; my feeling of well-being melts into thin air, I am afraid, I am so afraid, but I need to see... 'I want to go away!' Yet I can't resist the lure. The silence is absolute; I walk round the coffin (the men are still marching on). 'But I don't want to see.' 'You must!' I am weak with fear, I want to avert my eyes, I shake. Don't push me. Some force compels me to look. 'What? It is I myself! Myself! I can't, how horrible! This is madness!' My features are cruel: my head twisted in pain, my eyes staring, rolling, lost in infinity. For a moment I am unsure of myself, my thoughts. Everything shocks and disturbs me. 'And if that is really *me*... am I then *another*?' I have to run away. The coffin halts and the ghostly crowd melts away, silently, in waves... Death has me spellbound so that I can't move. A lead weight falls on me, pinning me to the ground. I struggle desperately to free myself, to break the chains of that deathly silence. 'Let go of me! Let go of me!' At first I want to cry out, but the breath doesn't move in my throat, there is no sound. I'm suffocating. Finally I let out a superhuman cry which tears at my breast. The crowd vanishes into thin air; the street is empty, full of sun; only me there, left in the coffin. It's me, it's me! Leave me alone! I know that I am really here in the coffin, me, dead and alone. I'm not split in two as I was just now, I'm *just one self, me*. And again I can't cry out. I am dead. 'Take me! Take me!' But how can anybody hear? The air is opaque; it's getting dark. Is night falling? Will I be here for ever? I feel a boundless terror. The darkness is awful. I can feel the coffin

JOSÉ RODRIGUES MIGUÉIS

melting away under my weight. I can't see anything. I'm stiff as if I were dead. Where am I? But I am alive; my heart is beating. I fell an intense longing for that warm sun, that smiling springtime, and the joy of being myself again.

I need time to come out of my stupor. Could I have really died and awoken in the world of darkness? I make a great effort to compose myself again; the far-off, regular ticking of a clock brings me back to reality. I get my bearings. All sorts of terrible thoughts run through my head. I jump out of bed – Luisa is still sleeping – and bend over the spotless white bed of my son; he too is sleeping, peacefully, between the curtains which fall in folds like the wings of the angels who guard him. His little soul must dwell in a blissful, higher part of this world, although his poor, feeble body lies here, burning in its stubborn, long drawn-out fever.

And his future? He is so patient, so good, this boy. He never asks for anything, not like certain selfish little brats who cry all night. It's enough to tell him to go to sleep for him to do so. And to think that he will have to hear the dreadful words: 'Be off with you, your father was a thief!' (I clench my fists on the bars of his innocent bed.) They will shut their doors in his face, fearful and contemptuous. 'Quite likely he's worse than his father who was a crook through and through...'

And me, good God, dead or in exile, of no use to the poor boy whose life I've defiled since the cradle. Not even if I took my own life could I save him; my death would just be the final disgrace. I must live. I tell myself again: 'I must save him, I must save *both of them*!'

By the time I go back to bed dawn has broken. My heart beats more calmly; my resolve is firmer.

XI

'I find you much changed, Renato,' he tells me. 'You seem different. You're depressed, why don't you do something about it? Take a few days off, rest a while; you're working too hard. We can get somebody in to cover for you.'

The sleepless nights, the nightmares, my ceaseless labours have taken their toll: my weariness is visible. Every morning I find another white hair; there is a permanent sad furrow on my brow, which has an unhealthy yellowish tinge. The miserable state I'm in has caught his eye. I look at him, hiding my feelings: does he suspect something, or is it because he's really concerned that he talks to me like this? Who can say? I don't want to say anything more which might attract his attention.

'No, sir,' I reply, 'it's nothing, I'm perfectly... perhaps it's a touch of anaemia. Or a kind of depression which comes sometimes, nothing more. It'll go away.'

No, I don't need anyone else working here. I don't want snoopers. I'm not having anyone in here, even though I'm going to have to increase my own efforts a hundredfold.

And supposing I told him the real reason for my depression? No, no. Certainly he's going to want to see the little boy, and then? He's bound to notice the absence of the furniture we had in the 'good old days'. (How long ago that seems!) The house is so dreary now. The flowers on the balcony have faded from neglect.

'I haven't seen your little boy for such a long time,' he says. 'And how is your wife?'

'They're fine, in great form,' I reply, without meeting his gaze which I sense is resting on me.

'He must be quite a little man by now.'

'A little man, yes,' I say.

I am bound inescapably – as if by a hoop – to these pictures in my mind. But why is Nogueira looking at me so insistently? He seems nervous; he's a lot more serious than before. I have to let him see me cheerful and relaxed. How much longer will this wretched farce go on? His questions embarrass and confuse me. I stutter and stammer, my answers are unintelligible, I put off indefinitely sorting out certain problems relating to the cash account. 'I just don't understand how...'

Previously he was much less concerned about the things which now seem to obsess him. He sticks out his lower lip, scratches his little beard, reads all the letters and asks me countless questions: 'You need my help, don't you?'

I'm afraid of him; my knees knock every time he asks me something.

I enter the office and see him bent over the books, files open everywhere, his glasses glinting above the line which furrows his forehead, his face red with the effort of concentration: 'Good morning. You're in early.'

'Just some matter I've been mulling over,' I reply.

I turn white, distraught. 'There's no question: he knows.' I hang up my hat and silently, like a wraith, I tiptoe over to my desk. My work obliges me to leave home earlier and earlier every day, half dead with apprehension. But he too comes in earlier every day! I sense that he's got hold of the thread of this story; it will take some doing to get to the end of it. I haven't the courage to open my mouth. If I did confess, then perhaps I could still be saved. But then, perversely, fear turns to hate. 'Thief! Wretch!' The desire returns, the desire to stab him in the back, as he bends over his books, defenceless, the nape of his neck exposed...

And then what? I'm going mad; as if I could do it!

Meanwhile one day when we're face to face, I feel my

JOSÉ RODRIGUES MIGUÉIS

muscles tighten with a murderous impulse I can't hold back. I grip the top of the table as if it were some kind of life-raft. His voice seems far away: 'What's the matter with you? What's the matter with you? Don't you feel all right? You're so pale, the sweat is rolling down your face. Sit down, man. Good God, your face...'

The room, the furniture whirl around me; the table that I'm holding onto shakes violently and Nogueira stares at me, terrified: 'Have a drink of cold water.'

I sit down and, as if to appease him, slowly drink the water which he anxiously offers me from the glass in his hand; he is at once sympathetic and stern, like a father. I am like a little boy, meek in his presence. 'I could do it now; if only I...' I shake off the drops which have spilled onto my tie and waistcoat. 'Go home, go and rest,' he urges. 'You're far from well.'

Oh, he's even more calculating than I am. He knows everything, knows that this way of his is killing me slowly from fear, and he doesn't say a word. He wants to make me confess.

The sound of his voice briefly cools the force of my anger.

For days I've been feeling horribly weary. Supposing I just called him a few names and then disappeared, and thought no more about the theft, or about my family, or about these evil spirits of mine. I must contain myself: I have to follow this torture through to the end. But when will I be able to pay back what I have stolen? Where will I get the strength from?

Man has within him more extraordinary strengths than he is aware of and it's only in the midst of struggle that he can draw on them. Would they were only harnessed to the good!

Winter passed.

The little boy has finally got to the stage of convalescence. In the heavens and on the earth there are signs of spring; from time to time a bird, singing, flies in front of the windows where the sun beats down. The doctor, who always comes early to visit this little stunted flower, before going on to see his older patients, smiles and says paternally through his beard: 'This little ship is safe.'

Luisa listens to him, her eyes swollen with tears, nervously playing with her white apron, and blushes from head to foot.

Now the nights and days pass more easily. A breath of hope and renewal helps us to rebuild our lives. The sun, pale and cheerful, smiles through the windows and the little chatterbox in his peaceful, pink bedroom comes out of his fever.

'He's like a little flower that has survived a great fire.'

'Quiet now,' says his mother, 'don't talk. Look at the bogey man.' Tenderly she holds him close. He realises she's just joking and smiles gratefully. I want to smother the child with kisses but as he almost disappears under the bedclothes I hardly dare touch him for fear of hurting him.

My confidence is coming back; it was nothing but a nightmare. It's finished. My life is beginning again; all I need is the courage.

But what about Nogueira? Why don't I just tell him everything, come straight to the point, quite calmly, and ask his forgiveness and enough time to repay what I have stolen? I'll say: 'Mr Nogueira, I've taken advantage of the confidence you showed me: I've been stealing from you.' And then: 'I'm prepared to pay back whatever you've lost.'

But this moment of resolution never comes: in front of the old man my crime seems monstrous, ignoble, not to be redeemed by confession. So I redouble my efforts, I can't rest until I have rebuilt our lives.

Time passes so swiftly, I hardly notice it. I'm barely conscious of the tumult which is Carnival. The spell of fine weather hasn't lasted long and one day the rains come again and the wind sighs sadly in the high windows of the house.

'We're going to have bad weather for Easter,' says Luisa.

JOSÉ RODRIGUES MIGUÉIS

'What a shame. If it gets any better we might take him out somewhere.'

'If only we could,' I reply.

She sews by the window while the little one, whose convalescence drags wearily on, plays on the bed with dolls and postcards. We look out through the window at the rain cascading down the roofs of our neighbours, beating, steaming, driven by the wind. To her the rain means poetry and sadness. She stops sewing and looks at her son; after a while she whispers her fears to me: 'Supposing he doesn't get better soon.'

'Bah, what rubbish! We'll get things right,' I tell her. 'Do you think I waste my time thinking such nonsense? Your fears are just old wives' tales.'

The poor woman naturally thinks that 'getting things right' simply means that we shall fill this bare house with furniture again and return to the gentle monotony of earlier days. If she only knew; if one day I could tell her about my burden... but she never asks a single question, not even about this futile life I have been leading for months now.

With the onset of the rain and as the city assumes a gloomy, dejected air, still clammy despite the foul weather, Nogueira suddenly resumes his questioning, demanding items in the budget, entries in the ledger, bills, documents from the safe, sifting through the cheque books and the books in the warehouse.

One day as he is coming up to the office he passes me on the stairs with a fellow whose face rings a bell; I stop and turn back to make sure, so that when he gets to the landing the light from below shows me who he is: he is the clerk that I had sacked earlier. I have to lean against the wall so as not to fall. 'Be brave, be brave! It won't be long now.' Not a word did Nogueira say to me about this visit. It's therefore certain that... And why does he spend so long talking to the boy who works in the warehouse? He gets letters he doesn't let me read and which he takes his time to reply to; he rummages through the correspondence. Certain pages of the books seem to fascinate him: he spends ages looking at them, whistling softly and drumming his fat, be-ringed fingers on the table. I don't know which is the more oppressive – his silence, or my own. They are both unbearable. My silence is a confession, the clearest of all. Indeed, there is no help for it: so when, with a huge effort I manage to conquer my fear, I bend over him to ask:

'Is something wrong? It could be a mistake of mine...'

'No, it's nothing really; just a little matter,' he replies, his voice curt, dry and cold.

I don't know whether suffering dulls our moral sense. I do know that I am suffering, but I can't otherwise explain how I can subject myself to torture like this, to so much humiliation.

The days are all alike, the nights just like the days. Time is like molten lead being poured continuously over me. I no longer try – I can't – to seem light-hearted and confident at home. I can't even get my sums right. I'm incapable of expressing myself logically and clearly. Do you know what I would really like to do? I just want to run away, find somewhere to be alone and write down everything tormenting me. But I'm being dragged along helplessly, like someone who's drunk. Not even the strength which drove me to the crime returns to help me. I'm carried along by the current, my arms open wide. Oh, it can even be enjoyable, almost sensual at some moments, to live like this with your conscience in abeyance. If somebody stuck a gun in my chest I would just shrug: I don't really care whether I live or die. It's funny that I now feel no anger against this old man who, by turns, I have liked or loathed. He fiddles with the books and I look at him indifferently. I seem to have lost my senses. I begin to think: 'I want him to know.'

　　　　　　　　　　JOSÉ RODRIGUES MIGUÉIS

'Easter's early this year,' says Luisa.

'I don't know, I suppose you're right,' I reply. 'I don't even know what day it is.'

'But it's almost Easter already, man!'

'My brain's stopped working,' I say.

When I get to the office Nogueira says: 'This year we're going to close the office for a few days – from Tuesday to Easter. But come in if you want to; we've a lot to talk about.'

So he knows everything; only a blind man would not have seen all the mistakes, the lies...

XII

It's exactly ten o'clock in the morning.

I stroll along in leisurely fashion, open the outer gate then the door, and go in, completely at ease. 'What a gloriously sunny morning,' I think. 'How good it would be to go out into the countryside, in good spirits, to spread a white cloth on the grass, set out the glasses, knives and forks, open the hamper and take out a nice fat chicken, still warm and golden, see the wine sparkling in the sun, as ruby red and translucent as a shower of jewels. The little one, the little one playing. "Don't run," says his mother. "Let him," say I. "It will do him good, cooped up in the house all day." "I don't want him out in the sun." "Well then, give him a sun hat," I say. "Here, take this hat; off you go, have a run about, but don't go too far."'

'Good morning.'

Ah, I had forgotten. Standing at the entrance to the office, his arms across his chest, his eyes screwed up, he is looking at me through his gold-rimmed glasses. I return his gaze with interest: his little beard rests severely on his tie where a topaz is glinting.

The office: on top of the tables there are books open at particular pages, bills, invoices, files. The safe is open, a bunch of keys hanging from the lock. Yes sir, it's an impressive arrangement, everything silently laid out like this. Yes indeed, sir, full marks. Is that all? I understand; let's go to it. Everything seems to be looking at me, questioning me, proving a point. Well, lads, this is for me.

At last. I feel no fear.

Absolutely no fear. My expression must be one of relief, of

freedom. I don't have to pretend any longer, which means... No, my expression says everything. I myself have nothing to say; why should I? Haven't the documents spoken? So then, it's all been said.

Well? He looks at me – this is a fine thing – his eyes almost closed. That's no use, my fine fellow; it doesn't bother me at all. What I want most of all is just to close my eyes, to fall asleep and forget everything. I bow my head. And he, isn't he going to say anything? Is he waiting for me to speak? My nerves don't even bother me. Should I deny it? How could I, and what good would it do?

But what peace. Someone goes by outside in the street, whistling. In my mind I follow his footsteps. Maundy Thursday! A deadly silence bears down on both of us in this yellow office with its low border of old tiles. It seems more cheerful today. This peace relaxes me, I feel as though I'm going to burst out laughing crazily.

'Is there something?'

'You know very well what all this means, don't you? I've been making inquiries for a long time now; you saw what I was doing. But not a single word; your cynicism is beyond words. I had guessed, I saw something in you, I don't know what. But no, I said to myself, he's an honest chap. But, in the end, it was clear: you've been robbing me, robbing me of more than thirty thousand escudos, you thief! You're just a thief, nothing more than a cheap crook.'

All these words, son, just for me. I am quite indifferent to his insults. And indeed, red-faced, with his Brazilian accent, he almost seems ridiculous, poor old Nogueira. What are you waiting for, do you want me to get down on my knees, howling, begging your forgiveness? That would be good, affecting perhaps, but I can't. I can't. My impassiveness disconcerts him. Dear Lord, now he's going to tell me the whole story, all the obvious things, like something out of *True*

Confessions. As if I don't know. Enough is enough. He's been through hell. Well then, goodbye. And my son; what the devil has he to do with this? His illness, the furniture we pawned. Oh, Mr Nogueira, it's not worth getting worked up like this. Don't shout, don't shout any more!

'I ought to have a couple of policemen here, you understand, to take you straight to the jug. But I'm not going to do it; I still have enough magnanimity to save you; but I'm not doing this for you, do you hear, it's for them, for your wife, poor thing, and for your son. I do have a heart. Maybe I'm wrong; I would never have had you down as a thief who would rob me like this, like a traitor, a miscreant whom I brought into my own house. Oh Lord, there's no punishment in heaven for this kind of thing. A man I befriended, to whom I entrusted everything, to whom I was a father...'

(It could have been worse, Mr Nogueira, much worse.)

I can see clearly that it pains him to speak. It's he who wants to cry and all I want to do is laugh!

'A man can always redeem himself – if he gets help and he truly wants to. You weren't bad, you weren't. It was someone... tell me truthfully, did someone put you up to it? Answer me!... Don't answer then and the devil take you. Imagine it,' he laughs bitterly, 'imagine it, in the face of this shamelessness and I'm still talking about moral regeneration. And you,' his laugh becomes painful, 'and you, what do you say to that. Say something, damn it! Lift your head and look at me, at least show some backbone.'

What does he want me to say? I don't feel any kind of gratitude. He mumbles something and paces about furiously in the narrow space.

'And this happened to me, Lord, to me. This scoundrel to whom I held out my hand, to whom I blindly entrusted everything. Your life – oh yes, yes, I know well enough, but you'll have to pay, oh yes.' And on he goes. He insults me and mutters words I can't make out, with his fist clenched in rage behind his back, ready to hit me, driven frantic by indifference – or by his own excessive forebearance: 'You're not even ashamed. Don't you even think of those poor wretches back at home?'

The poor books can hardly avoid the blows he rains down on them. A thin dust rises and the motes dance in the air. What? What is all this in aid of? Is he going to hit me? Well then... he seizes my arm and shakes me, asking how I came to this miserable state: 'Who made you do it? Who was it? I want you to tell me.'

'Only me, only me, sir.' (Me, and the *other*. But who could know?) In a few words I tell him how I did it.

He looks at me in astonishment, shaking his head. For him it's all so unexpected, so absurd.

'A year; I'll give you a year to repay what you've stolen. And within a week I want guarantees – some suitable guarantor, whoever you want. Not a day more: a week. And if you don't you know exactly what will happen – prison. Shame, a trial, the disgrace of your family. Do you hear me? I get the feeling you're not listening. You must be completely mad, mad.'

He storms about in his shirtsleeves, sweating, kicking the chairs and table legs. I begin to find it ridiculous: me – the thief, the wretch – here motionless, defenceless, uncommunicative, like a worthless wet rag hung, dripping, from a nail in the corner of the hall.

Then suddenly, I don't know how, I open my mouth and venture to tell him, speaking humbly, hesitantly, like someone reading out his lesson, about my son's illness, the sacrifices we made, the furniture we pawned. I speak mechanically, using contrived phrases borrowed from books, phrases I had formed a long time ago and which I was sure I had forgotten. I don't know myself. I didn't think I was capable of speaking like that, in this tearful, cringing voice like

JOSÉ RODRIGUES MIGUÉIS

a common crook. My words must be oozing cowardice and treachery. Nogueira listens to me, in irritation to begin with, but then little by little more calmly. No, he is not a stone; his heart rules his head. His lips tremble when I speak about the poor little child 'who is not to blame for my mistakes'.

I have finished. We are alone. The morning, clear and bright, proclaims a pleasant Easter after all. An uncommon calm augments the silence in the streets while the sun softly gilds the interior of the office, with its mustiness and its odour of coal-tar soap. Once again a deep, vibrant silence draws us closer. He paces up and down, his arms behind him, lightly whistling a waltz which was fashionable twenty years ago. I hear the familiar ticking of the clock with its hidden pendulum. In the end nothing has changed. Life is standing still, only the clock reminds us that time is passing. A tear has sprung from my eye for a moment while I was speaking and rests contritely on my cheek. The music of my own words has managed to calm me completely; there seems to be no sadness between the two of us.

But this is hateful, my cynicism, this indifference which has taken possession of me. I feel vaguely sleepy; how good it would be to sleep. I think the shadow of a smile flits across my mouth. My face must now be horrible, fool that I am. Yes, yes, I do feel relieved, now at last. Deep down after this indescribable, solitary torment I feel quite at ease with myself. I breathe deeply – how good it feels. It's just as if I had escaped from some great danger. And now? But I have to fight this foolishness: clearly I have no right to feel so unperturbed.

No, I want to resist this feeling of well-being, of great peace which threatens me at such a hazardous moment; I want to fight it. What a wretch! What I needed was some frightful physical torture. No, I'd rather *see*. I want to see my shame in the clear light of day, I want to suffer, to repent. I search through my memories of certain things which torment me, I dwell fiercely on my crimes, I call myself names. I go even further: I call to mind the court, the prison, the public display of my disgrace, being cut off from everything, the privation. But nothing, nothing, not a flicker of sorrow. All this means nothing to me, nor does the future. Inwardly I compare myself to certain amoral creatures, insensitive in every way to their disgrace. I go even further: the misery of my son, insulted, forced to beg, humiliated and reviled in every way. Nothing, nothing, none of this is anything but hypocrisy, from the abjectness of my bearing to my affected words and borrowed phrases – everything calculated for effect, as in a play. What a wretch! I don't think, I just talk to myself. I am hateful. I heap onto my own head all the fury, all the anger, all the loathing I can summon. There have been robbers who have shown nobility of soul, but not me. I am a scoundrel who deserves every possible punishment. I stand by, impassive, while these things happen. I have never considered the welfare of others, that's the honest truth. My hopelessness, which in my internal wrangling I frequently tried to pretend was the product of some vague ideal, was simply the result of my own inability to be happy, to achieve or succeed in anything.

And what if I had been luckier in life's game of chance? But no. And then I have wasted the life of that poor woman; I have had a child only to disgrace and abandon him; I have robbed the man who thought he would make something of me. Despair, hunger, everlasting pain, disillusionment; and I don't even feel remorse. To tell the truth I am afraid of the moral desolation in which I now find myself. I would like to weep, fall to my knees in lamentation, wail, kiss the hands of this vigorous, noble old man who has not delivered me into the hands of the police – but I can't, I can't. (And I still want to laugh.) If I tried to do it, it's clear that my gesture would come out all wrong, all too calculated. My God, how did I get like this? Perhaps it's just that I, who have suffered too, have

　　　　　JOSÉ RODRIGUES MIGUÉIS

now become oblivious to suffering.

And while he paces up and down, lost in thought, and the shimmering pool of sunlight slips across the clean floor and then onto the tables, in deadly silence, I want to retreat inside myself, to some inaccessible depths, down to the last dregs of self-respect. Respect, yes, or rather the self-esteem which every man needs to live. Although this honourable old man has already told me that he isn't going to lodge a complaint against me because he believes in the rehabilitation of criminals, although he has assured me that everything has been forgotten and that I can return to work tomorrow, I still haven't got the self-esteem. It's all over. Rather a life sentence than this freedom that I can't stand. Hammering at my heart is like hammering at a tomb. While my son was ill I might even have believed; but now, now there is no salvation for me. And Nogueira still believes. I know there's no help for it. I am my own shipwreck. I am ready. There will be neither pardon nor punishment.

Nogueira has paused; his penetrating gaze pierces me like an X-ray: 'I knew about the problem your little one had.' What next? He hesitates. Oh my God, he's started off again. Will this never end? And if he were to forgive me? That would be even worse. I have to suffer. Will he come to see the little boy? He's even capable of... But hey now, here comes something interesting.

Once again he bends over the books. It's as if he's a different person. Maybe he needs to remind himself of what I've done, to harden his heart so that he doesn't go soft on me. 'What are you waiting for?' asks the unruly, ironic voice in me.

Time now oozes slowly, like a thin trickle of oil. Nogueira, his glasses on his forehead, scrutinises the documents, sniffing, uttering unintelligible noises from time to time. He nods his head and bangs out the rhythm of a march on the table.

Now he stands in front of me: 'Within a month – how's

that? – I want those guarantees. And then you have a year, don't forget: *a year*. Right, that's enough said. The matter's settled. Consider yourself dismissed. It's just possible that later we can fix something up in Brazil, in Manaus, perhaps.'

Brazil, that dream of mine! Oh well, that's just wonderful!

Now he's giving me advice, talking about my son, about the future: 'Ah, if only I had a son. A son, sir, is an obligation that we take on for the future; we have to honour it. He is like a mirror in which our blemishes are reflected. Don't have any illusions: it's only because of him that I'm doing this; without the boy you would now be in prison.'

The words wash over me, I don't take them in, they fall unheeded. My weariness is infinite; my legs are giving way under me. How good it would be just to let myself keel over on the floor and forget everything. And this strange caress of something shining, I don't know where it comes from, it attracts me. My eyes wander. There it is! My heart beats wildly. The knife! The long burnished blade of the paper knife lying on the table. I can't take my eyes off it. A thousand vivid shafts of light, like the colours of the rainbow, caress my eyes: a mysterious world, brightly coloured and gleaming, where I would love to enter, becoming invisible, vibrant as an atom. That sliver of metal attracts me: it's so slim, I want to feel it cool in my hands, on my forehead, on my neck. I tremble. The notion of the caress of that ice-cold blade slowly penetrating my flesh, ripping my nerves, muscles, arteries, produces in me a state of drowsy, sensual well-being, a stillness which is almost absolute. My eyes close in sleep, softly, under the command of that vital reflex. I smile at it lovingly. Even with my eyes shut I can still see it. The office turns ponderously about me. Oh how good it would be to feel cold metal in my blood... and the glittering... a thousand coloured shafts of light, spiralling like a vortex of light, dance in my head.

'... ready. Now go and do your duty like a man and show

JOSÉ RODRIGUES MIGUÉIS

that you deserve the name of father. Goodbye.'

With some difficulty he slips his right hand into his trouser pocket. Then unhurriedly, doggedly, he crosses the office and goes out into the lobby. I follow him slowly, as if sleep-walking. He raises his hand to the bolt and from the shadows he says: 'We all make mistakes at least once in our lives; for many it's life itself which prevents them making good the wrong they have done.' He sighs, looks at me and then turns his gaze away, and says solemnly: 'I'll have to go and see that son of yours, poor thing.'

He slowly unlocks the old dark green iron door, opens the outer door and gestures to me. I walk past him with my head bent, without looking back, like someone leaving a prison – I've had enough of that carry-on. The steps are in shadow; from there below comes the foul smell of cats and rubbish. Where am I going? I go down the first flight, my hat in my hand, hesitating, as if I had forgotten something. I have the feeling that he is still standing in the doorway, watching me from behind. 'Remember that today is Maundy Thursday,' he says. 'I wish you a Happy Easter.'

What? What is he saying? Was it he who spoke? What a voice! I can hear the noise of the old bolts as he closes the door. I'm not sure what to do. I stand there alone. I walk down a few steps and then stop, uncertain. Those words... what then? I feel as though I've forgotten something; I don't know what but I've forgotten something. I'm absolutely sure of it; I have to do something. Bowing my head I turn and climb the steps again. 'A Happy Easter... a Happy Easter...' Was he making fun of me? I paused by the grill; what have I come back for? What was it I forgot? I'd better look; really, I'd better look. For the first time I notice that the bell-pull is knotted in several places. Calmly, decisively, I give it a firm tug. Footsteps... here he comes; and again the noise of the bolts. Through the bars of the grill I see Nogueira, looking at me with astonishment in his eyes. Suddenly he seems much older.

'It's me.'

'What? Have you forgotten something? Do you want to speak to me?'

I nod. There's no doubt that I have forgotten whatever it was. I go in slowly with the tentative steps of someone who isn't sure what he's looking for. A dumb agitation is beginning to stir in me, an irritation almost, that I can only attribute to those words with their – I don't know exactly – lingering, cryptic sense of irony. The blood surges through my whole body, as if I was being licked by flames. We go back in, and he follows me, silently, passively. Everything is the same as it was a short while ago. But something, I don't know what, has changed.

What I am doing surprises me and fills me with curiosity. Why have I come back? Meanwhile the voice inside me repeats: 'It's out of the question that he will forgive you; he's going to send you to prison.' Then all at once I look at the table. Everything else is blotted out; only the glittering blade is staring at me. I smile at him. How beautiful the marble handle is!

'What do you want?' Nogueira asks me, apprehensively. 'Tell me what you want?'

He moves closer to me. My hand reaches out towards the table... I grab the knife and somehow Nogueira and I find ourselves face to face. 'What do you want from me? What's going on?'

I don't know what I'm doing. I shudder; I close my eyes and I *see*. I smile gently. It's not me, it's someone else who is doing this. I don't know whether I say anything to him, but I shall never forget his astounded gaze nor the way he moved his head to bid me *no*. I run my fingers along the knife's narrow blade. Just to feel the cold metal gives me a sweet, piercing, sensual joy. My fingers run along its edge as far as

JOSÉ RODRIGUES MIGUÉIS

the point and I feel that I too am like the knife, long, slender, sharp, I too am a dagger. 'It's all a dream, I'm just dreaming, this is just absurd, absurd.' Why should I fight it? I'm just dreaming. But a savage curiosity... Let's see: is this just one more nightmare to add to the others. Is that someone's name I hear? Possibly; perhaps it's my son's name, the one with which the old man is beseeching me for the last time. Everything goes blank. 'A Happy Easter... a Happy Easter...' I haven't enough energy to think; nor has he the time to say anything more. I am dumb, deaf, devoid of feelings. The knife and his face, nothing else. I grab the collar of his jacket with my left hand and he grasps me round the wrist with both hands, shaking, his eyes closed.

With my right hand I strike him swiftly in the neck, two, three times – I don't know for sure. His quick red blood gushes out, soaking his jacket and shirt. His eyes are still closed, he sighs deeply almost with contentment. He lets go my arm. He is motionless. Peacefully he slips down the wall until he is almost sitting, his head against the still open safe, and the flow of blood drenching his clothes and running onto the shiny clean floor where it collects between the floorboards.

I put the knife down next to him. I wipe my hands, which the blood hasn't even stained, on a towel, set my hat firmly on my head and with a naturalness which astonishes me, and the calmness of someone who is following an order he cannot defy, I close the door and the outer gate on Nogueira's body, on my past, and go down the steps in leisurely fashion. An unreal silence... What beautiful weather, what beautiful sunshine. It would be so good to go for a walk in the country-side, stretch out my aching arms on the cool grass and look up at the sky through the fresh young leaves of the laurels and poplars. A Happy Easter. I feel *free*. I start to walk. A veil falls over my conscience. What am I going to do? I wander about aimlessly for a long, long time.

XIII

or such a long, long time. It is already late when I feel
an overwhelming need to go and see Nogueira, to
explain to him at leisure how I abused his trust. I want
to ask his pardon, thank him for his kindness, say some final,
moving words that I just can't get out of my head. I feel at last
a remorse which reveals to me the human depths of my
heart. I feel almost happy that I am suffering in this way, that
I have some notion of the wrong I have done to others.

The last memory – that was it, it was the moment when *he*
closed the door. Then – but I have to talk about him; at this
time I'll have to go to his house, of course. I cross the whole
city on foot, up to Avenidas Novas. Night is slowly falling.

His house; I hesitate. Is it this one here, or that one? No,
I've got it wrong. It feels as though I'm just coming out of a
long drunken delirium. Everything is closed. Why don't I go
in here. I open the gate, cross the garden, go up four steps and
peer through the glazed door. Beyond me I can hear the rain
dropping on the leaves. I bang on the door. On the first floor
there's an open window.

'Mr Nogueira, Mr Nogueira,' I shout.

There's no reply. Then an old maidservant appears at the
window. 'Ah, it's you,' she says.

'That's right, it's me.'

'Do you want to come in? Wait there, I'm coming down.'

'Is the boss in?'

'No, he hasn't come home yet. I'm a bit worried: he's
usually home a lot earlier. Weren't you with him at the
office?'

'At the office? Yes, in the morning...' Her question makes

me blanch. Why wasn't I there in the office the whole day? 'Good night,' I call, but the old woman says something that I don't want to hear and I leave in some haste.

In my breast my heart is bursting. I go back to the Baixa where the streets and avenues are bathed in deep blue shadows. I run, crying, I know not where. I'm in a hurry. I ask myself if it is remorse which is making me cry. I don't know. I don't know anything. There is something broken in pieces inside me, and I am crying. My tears make me feel better, comfort me, almost make me happy. This heaviness in my heart and in my temples goes away little by little. My agitation subsides. It's such a long time since I have cried like this. My tears flow continuously and somehow I'm proud of them. From being a small boy I've always thought of tears as a badge of shame and suffering. If I'm crying now it's because I'm suffering.

This café... I'm going somewhere I haven't been for years. I open the outer door: they're still the same old frosted windows.

In the old days in this place, which was almost always closed to the prying eyes of the street, I used to meet a group of lads with whom I would drink beer. Under this roof and within the painted, dirty green walls, with their tarnished, pitted mirrors, life seemed to me stupid and boring but at least bearable. One day a change of job and my marriage took me away from this narrow circle; a new life beckoned and I left my single companions of those days. But perhaps some of them...

I open the door. The muggy atmosphere is thick with smoke; it flattens the shapes and the faces. The light is sad, yellowish. All the tables are full. Over everything there hangs the continuous murmur of conversations which seem to be coming through the wall. With a great effort I study one after the other the faces bent over the tables; I don't recognise any of them. Glasses clink. What am I doing here? It's so many years. Now I feel like a stranger. The buzz of conversation and the dim atmosphere makes me dizzy. My eyes flit vaguely over the pink marble of the table tops, the mirrors, the artificial palms, forever green and pointless in their brightly painted flowerpots. Nobody notices me; I both dread and yet long to meet someone, a friend to whom I could tell... I no longer have any friends; in truth I never had any. But this doesn't stop me. What brought me here was an absurd desire to reach out to someone. In me the conflict between my desire and my feeble resolve grows more intense.

There, left behind on top of this table lies a crumpled newspaper which looks as though it has served its purpose. Red letters – *Le Journal... Le Journal.* Crudely I say the name. My deadened spirit seizes on the coloured word as if on a toy and begins to play around with it. Words possess hidden, mysterious meanings which I turn over in my mind. *Le Journal.* I've no idea what time it is.

A waiter comes by and says something. I leave, beating back my longing. The door closes behind me with a thud. Once again I find myself among indifferent, unyielding buildings and the passing crowd. Everybody's going home. Dark shapes hastening, and the confused sound of footsteps on the ground. The dusk is dying into night. The sky with its low clouds against the reddish walls seems to be an unnaturally deep blue.

Le Journal... Le Journal...

This rhythm soothes me. I begin again to roam the streets, in desolation, without direction or purpose. If only something unforeseen would happen to wrench me out of my torpor.

'Luck, sir, this means good luck!' From beneath a tattered black shawl comes the hand of an old woman, scrawny and wrinkled. The white, dog-eared lottery tickets flutter, her voice is uneven and toneless. 'This will bring you luck, sir,' she says. 'Buy a ticket and do yourself a favour.'

'Leave me alone!'

I feel an inhuman hatred, not for her but for her servility – the servility of the weak which is the first victory of the strong. What use is it? Just to suffer? It would be more help to her to finish her off. Her muffled, loathsome voice sobs insistently: 'Only a few coppers; you never know your luck. Help me to live!'

I look sideways at her furiously, and she, misunderstanding my look, stretches out her wrinkled, trembling hand again, and grabs the sleeve of my jacket with her loathsome snake-like fingers: 'Look, it's 2713.'

I shudder. Devil take her. Thirteen... I can't stand thirteen; I swear by its malign power. I shake off her revolting touch. 'Make yourself scarce, woman,' I cry pitilessly, almost as if about to strike her. I know well enough I could have beaten her savagely. The old woman makes off, muttering.

But I can't stop thinking about the number. It burns behind my eyes, to the core of my brain; it covers the red headlines of the newspaper like a neon sign in the dark depths of the night. I try desperately to fight it back. There are some images you can't get rid of, no eyelids shield the eyes of the imagination. The numbers keep coming back, dancing, changing shape, mocking and alive. It is as if they really existed inside me. I can't struggle any more; I can't see anything else, and so I surrender to this nightmare until the numbers leave me alone, satiated with their sport.

I am absolutely sure that this woman has some significance for me. It's a sign. The old woman... Only now do I realise she was a hunchback; a hunchback or a dwarf. The numbers whirl around fiendishly and an anguished sweat covers my brow. I open my eyes and turn back, but of course the old woman has disappeared around the corner, lost in the darkness amid the scurrying passers-by. I lean against the wall and wait. The numbers still dance before me. It's getting very strange: now, as if the chain which holds them has broken, they skip around at random; madly, with no logic they rise and fall, spin round like fireworks. How curious this is, how strange. Now they combine afresh – 7213 – 1273 – 1327 – now they go away, then they come back again, until, inexplicably, they fuse, join together, spinning round like crazy dancers: 13.

There is nothing except the number 13.

With the hated number etched on my retina I make myself walk much more quickly; I want to find narrower streets where there is less light and fewer people rushing about. In the shadows loom carts drawn by huge, placid mules which dip their heads into baskets to chew their food. People are gathering in the bars from which come the sounds of coarse voices and of dishes being banged together, and the acrid smell of burnt oil and fried fish. A blue smoke makes me look up at the sky: the night has closed in, and above the roofs blazes the roseate gleam of the city lights amidst the noisy confusion of car horns.

'Excuse me, I'm so sorry.'

A young man in a yellow coat bumps into me as he comes out of the tobacconist's to put up the shutters. Everywhere is closing. I go in and ask for a glass of water. There is a gaslight as in the old days. Now I recall the Baixa, so large and peaceful, lit in those days by the mournful green gaslights, the Baixa of my childhood, which seemed so homely and honest, so clean and circumspect. And I feel an intense longing. The shop has a low roof, old fittings in dark red mahogany. And in the back, behind the glass and fine clay jars on a white marble shelf, a useless, cracked mirror.

I'm calmer now. In the end everything, whatever it is,

changes simply by existing. It's not just I who have changed. *This* is another time. I have been sleeping, perhaps for many years.

'How much?' I ask.

'Nothing,' he replies.

'Thanks very much.'

Why is it? Only now do I remember. No wonder I thought I had forgotten something. I hear again that sweet little voice from deep within its pink bedroom, where everything is warm and cosy between the pure white curtains: 'Daddy, daddy, don't forget my sugared almonds for Easter.'

'My son...'

'Happy Easter.'

A sorrow pierces my breast like a dart. I don't have the courage! And if I ran away? or chose death? No, I couldn't leave him like that.

'Daddy, Daddy!'

'My son...'

A kiss; his little hands are so white: 'Your little hands are so cold,' I say. 'Put them under the bedclothes.' He smiles.

Everything is so white: his smile is white, too. Flowers? No, no, I don't want flowers, no. (But flowers.) 'How you do go on, my God! Take them away, take them away. Not flowers. Everything so white, sir, think of the impression. Your hands are so cold. Cover yourself up, cover yourself up; I'll tuck you in, here let me...' (But I'm rambling, clearly.)

'And the lights, why do you need all these lights in the daylight, sir? And so glaring! Blow them out, blow them out. I'll put them out.'

I blow. No, it's impossible, they won't go out. I rave, I suffer. 'Look at me,' I cry. 'Give me a kiss, a kiss! *Open your eyes!*'

I'm sweating profusely and I reach out my hands to fend off this apparition. I breathe deeply. It's nothing, it's just the nightmare which now assails me here in the street, the horror which has come back to haunt me in the guise of a delusion.

'It's going to have to be today.'

Today – what? I can't remember. Uncertain, I reach into my pockets. What am I looking for? My hands are numb with cold while my clothes are soaked with sweat.

'It's going to have to be today.' But what? *Today.* Where does this notion of coincidence come from? Coincidence, yes, but of what? I can't bear this anguish. My son is almost well, out of danger; the doctor thinks he can eat anything now and he happened to fancy some sugared almonds. That's the way children are and I have to do as he wishes. I have promised to bring him some but I have forgotten all about it during this awful day. What about money? I can't get this sweet little voice out of my head: 'Daddy, Daddy, don't forget!' It pulsates within my very soul, like a soft, ringing light – the only thing I have left – a pale light which hovers over the surface of the empty, baleful sea. How dark it is, my God, the night stifling and smothering the lights. I am shivering. Here they come, here come the crows again to tear my flesh. Shipwreck again? Oh, it's too much, this is pure deception. I struggle for breath, abandoned. Around me an immense swirl of water thunders and turns and my head swims. The greasy water glints, lit here and there by glow-worms and will o' the wisps. I'm drowning. Help, help! Through the immensity of the water comes the frail voice that I love. A deep core of calm in the midst of all this... Ah, how good it would be to let it take me to the bottom, to the bottom. Luisa, your smile; I smile as well. I can see you now: you're beautiful and your eyes are violet in the dusk. And the boy? I reach out my arms to you both, there you both are; how good it seems. Oh, my head is reeling; am I dying, perhaps?

There is a face leaning over me and its two dark staring eyes terrify me; it has a moustache. I close my eyes and turn to one side before opening them again. My face, my neck and collar are soaked. Two hands shake me by the shoulders. I see something white and shiny: it's a button, a metal button. Another and another. I open my eyes completely, though my eyelids are heavy, and see that it is a policeman. I look around: I am lying on the ground in the middle of a group of people – I see only legs and anxious faces.

My tongue feels heavy in my mouth.

'Say something! Are you all right, can you hear what I'm saying to you?'

I groan even though I'm in no pain, and nod.

Nothing makes sense. And now this: the image of a drop of blood which flows over something and then falls, making me shiver with cold.

I return to the Baixa. The sugared almonds? But what about money. Money? I can't go and steal any! I chew my fingers in anguish. What's happened to the nerve I used to have?

The river: the idea of throwing myself into the inky Tagus, flowing just a short distance away, silent and menacing, is so seductive that it makes me feel dizzy. I wouldn't even have to ask anyone! I feel to what extent I am alone in this life, in the isolation that I have lovingly built around me.

It's late; Luisa will be wondering why I'm late. The little boy will be asleep already, I'm sure; he must have asked for me many times in vain: 'Daddy, why doesn't Daddy come home?'

If only I could be done with all this.

I rummage through the pockets of my waistcoat and find a pen, the only possession I have other than the clothes I'm wearing.

'Let's see if you can get up then.'

I see that I am the object of a shameful curiosity and I

JOSÉ RODRIGUES MIGUÉIS

make a great effort to rise; many arms reach out to help me and lift me to my feet.

'Has he got up?'

'Give him a hand there.'

'Can you find your way home? Let's see.'

'Look at his face, poor soul.'

'He looks as though he isn't in his right mind.'

'I don't need help!'

'He's just had too much to drink.'

'Those eyes – they're frightening!'

'Maybe he's just starving; give him something to eat.'

'Come on, let him through. Would everybody please disperse now.'

There's a huge stir around me which bewilders me. What's the matter with me? Then suddenly I understand and the shame burns on my cheeks; I feel as though I want the ground to swallow me up but by dint of a huge effort I find some strength in my legs and with a sudden movement I break through the wall of curious spectators surrounding me. I am off, running, ashamed and terrified, hearing from behind me the murmur of comments and laughter; I turn the first corner and only stop when I'm far away in some almost empty street.

I'm feverish, delirious. I haven't eaten since morning and I've lost my senses. What's done is done, but now at least I am master of myself, thank God!

What's this? I can hear music; it's rather charming, I want to hear some more. Some fellows are hanging round the door of a shop. Since I'm in the shadows nobody notices me and I peep inside, under an arm leaning on the doorpost. It's one of those bazaars where they sell everything – knick-knacks, postcards, books, toys, sweets and things. Since it's a public festival the owner has stuck an old gramophone on the counter on top of a pile of boxes; pointing through the door is the reddish horn of its speaker, with white grooves, like a large, exotic but ridiculous flower. Further in, the shopkeeper peers from the shadows at his customers.

And there I stay, listening, foolishly.

A harsh, rough sound comes out of that flower. I know what it is: its an old fado, in the marialva style, which has been given a new lease of life in different rhythm. A woman is singing, but I can't make out the words. I can hear the chaotic hammering of one of those pianos that sounds like a mandolin, with some wild character playing it. I know it well, this little fado. Oh, what memories it brings back! I feel my life slip swiftly away from me and a sorrow, an inexplicable remorse. The thread of my thoughts snaps again and when I come round the voice has fallen silent. The group disperses, but for two men who talk in low voices near me, smoking and spitting on the cobbled pavement.

I set off on my wanderings again: 'Daddy, Daddy, don't forget!'

What can I do? I feel as if life is leaving me behind. What if I say to hell with it and tell all? I refuse: I can't bear their pitying looks. Not that. I pause. The lights form wavy lines on the deserted pavements. I check through my pockets and find a few coins which don't add up to anything at all. What's to be done? I button up my jacket and set off at a pace, full of misgivings.

If tomorrow... but the voice won't let me, it keeps whispering in my ear, so close, so alive, that I can feel its warm breath, almost as if his lips grazed my ear. 'Daddy, Daddy...' What's going to become of me. I can't go on, I can't. How can I go and see him while I'm in this miserable state. And what would I say to him, to her?

I run through the streets, now glistening with rain, and suddenly I find myself in front of the office, on the Cais da Areia. I'm going crazy. At this time it's completely deserted.

JOSÉ RODRIGUES MIGUÉIS

My heart pounds with joy. I return to the café I left a while ago and ask the waiter: 'You don't know me, it was a long time ago; what's his name, Bento, is he here?'

'No, there's no Bento here,' he says, eyeing me mistrustfully. 'Perhaps the manager...'

The manager comes, he seems sceptical but he tries the pen: it writes well but he has no use for it.

'It's an emergency,' I say, 'only until tomorrow; ten or fifteen escudos.'

'Very well then. Don't I know your face from somewhere?'

I grab the money and set off running like a madman. Some shops are just closing. I run into one and ask for the best sugared almonds; 'I want the best, you see they're for a little kid who's sick.'

I put the change in my pocket without checking it. My God, what elation. I can't think of anything else: I only want to see him smile. After that who knows if I will have the courage... I go along eagerly, happily. The house is so far away. I jump on a tram which is desperately slow. There is a cart across the tramlines so I decide to leap out onto the road. It's better to go on foot. I start running – the motion helps to calm my nerves. My mouth is open, my heart is beating wildly as I run down the avenues as if wolves were after me. My feet hardly touch the pavement; I am the projection of my own wishes. I don't see anyone passing, I run into people, perhaps I knock someone over. Some intimation of danger drives me on. Lisbon seems never-ending. 'My father, my Daddy...'

I turn the last corner. I stop short. A horrible anxiety overwhelms my heart, as if someone had got hold of me, cleaving my body in half. My life at this moment is a fateful conflict. I look at the house from afar: it's all dark. It's late; why have I stopped? And why am I in such a hurry? I go in and bound up the narrow staircase. Mechanically, as I usually do, I count the steps, the flights: 'First... second....' and breathe deeply like an exhausted dog.

'The third,' only one more now.

And then I miss my footing, the banister evades my grasp and I slip back – all in one quick movement – and fall helplessly against the iron rails of the staircase, sliding down the steps on my face. The little paper bag flies out of my hand and the weight of my body crushes it against the step as I fall. For a moment I lie outstretched, and as I try to get hold of something to help me stagger to my feet, though stunned, I hear the almonds crack on the step below.

There is the sound of voices, footsteps from a neighbour's house. I get up. I just want to throw myself head first into the black stairwell. My pain is so great I pummel my face and bite my fingers, unable to cry out or weep. The little one must be dreaming: 'Daddy, don't forget.' I choke with rage, I groan dumbly. I try to light some matches, I don't know why but my shaking hands won't let me. I lean against the wall and in a low voice, utterly cast down, I beg his forgiveness: 'My son, my little son.' The tears stream down my face.

But what's this? I'm trembling. Something touches me gently. I distinctly feel two small hands tenderly stroking my face. A voice, both near and distant, sweet and sad, fills my ears: 'Daddy, it's all right, it doesn't matter.'

What, oh no, it can't be. My God what does this mean? Am I going mad? One moment of painful dread; shivers run over my skin like electric shocks. A supernatural power enables me to rise above myself. Everything is headlong. I can hear voices, the muffled sound of steps, sobbing, groaning. At the same moment the whole day unfolds before me and I see again the crime I have committed. Something is crushing me, now. I wait... it's now. *A cry.* From up there, a shrill, sharp cry breaks out, piercing the dark with its strange light, a cry which lacerates, which rises like the jet of a fountain and

JOSÉ RODRIGUES MIGUÉIS

then dies slowly, vanishing, broken, sobbing, like water falling in drops, one by one. Then, hoarse, a death rattle. Someone faints; I recognise that voice though I never heard it cry out before: it's her. Now I understand. There is nothing more to be done up there. Everything is astonishingly clear.

Nogueira... well, that's over with. My self-possession in the face of this catastrophe is extraordinary. Before they open the doors I'd better go down. I can't feel anything. I'll never climb these steps again.

I stumble downstairs, through people with lights, running out onto the landing to help; they look at me silently. Something snaps beneath my feet. I go out into the street and breathe deeply. I start running aimlessly, dry-eyed, painlessly, as if it was I who had died and was miraculously, coldly, aware of what was happening around me. At this moment there's nothing I want, not even to die.

I never again return to the house.

More than this I can't remember: a few days later I was captured on the road to Mafra, half naked and starving. I didn't offer any resistance.

You, doctor, already know the rest of it.

Don't ask me anything else; it all happened just as I've said – it couldn't have been any other way, although I have my doubts sometimes and you may judge whether all this hasn't just been some kind of delusion.